MW01609797

Through These Eyes

M. ELAINE ELROD

Visit www.booksurge.com to order additional copies.

Cover Photography:
God's Eyes Photography
Owner: Dawn R. Mahler
917 Courtney Court SE, Concord, NC

Books can be ordered through amazon.com

Introduction

A few years back, I joined the Prayer Wall at my church and my prayer time was from 12:30 to 1:30 on Wednesday afternoons. I would always go in my little room and pray for the leaders of our country and for others. One day I decided to send an e-mail out to the people on my team at work. I felt sure someone had a need to bring before our Father. Much to my surprise, I received many requests.

I remember being so excited about people acknowledging their need and love for our Lord. Then I started getting e-mails to include others on my distribution list, and from there, it grew into my writing messages each week. This began a new thing between the Lord and me. When people would ask me where I came up with my words each week, I would tell them, "I am the messenger, He is the message." So many Wednesday's would come and I would pray for the words to write; but nothing came to me. Some of the ladies on my team

would say, "Give Him time, He'll tell you what to say."
They were right. Before I would have time to realize
what I was doing, my message was finished.

So many people are seeking the help of our Heavenly
Father and then some simply wish to praise Him for all
He's done for them. We should praise Him even when
we're up as well as when we're down.

"Through These Eyes" is a collection of real life stories,
quotes, and events that I, my family and my dearest
friends have lived. As the Lord gives me the words to
write, readers everywhere asked how I knew they had
experienced those events. I didn't, but God did. It took
me some time before I realized His words weren't just
for me; I was being led to write down what I heard.

Many readers requested that I consolidate my weekly
writings in book form so others might enjoy them as
well. While I can't thank each person, I would like to
thank my editors, Diane Ludman and Karen Faulkner
for their long hours slowly reading every word. Without
them this book would have taken much longer. They
are both good Christian women and they love the Lord
with all their heart.

I would also like to thank my family, especially my children. God used them to make it possible for me to see
clearly the love He has for all of us, the forgiveness he

showers on us and the happiness we bring to Him. He made each of us for His enjoyment, our children or families, if you will, are a special gift. We are to love and enjoy them, always protecting them from all harm, even until death.

Then I would like to thank each person I've had the opportunity of working with on this book. Some I was able to see each day, others, only over the phone. But it was always fun trying to picture how that person would look. We've all done it, only to find, boy were we wrong. These same people would send me requests for prayer and sometimes, they would tell me of something they had seen. Each one is so very special to me.

My hope and prayer is that you will find the writings, inspiring and uplifting. I know everything in this book was seen through my eyes but I want you to be able to visualize the same. I have received numerous emails and calls letting me know how certain messages hit home. And this is all I ask of our Savior, "Lord, I pray, one at a time, Savior, one at a time."

Table of Contents

Through My Eyes

Iwould like to know if you started your day off like I did, because I know I'm not alone in this, everything going haywire at five o'clock in the morning. First thing, my coffee wasn't strong enough, changed clothes four times...trying to get the right look you know...finally I'm on the road to work, look for a place to turn around, still have bedroom shoes on, now I won't have time to stop and purchase coffee. Get to work, get out change, go to vending machine, small cups only, not a problem I thought, I'll just go downstairs, I like that machine better anyway, IT'S BROKEN. At this point I started laughing, yesterday, last night and this morning I had been asking God to please give me the words to start writing today about attitude, what's the saying in Mark 8:18 *"Having eyes, do you not see? And having ears, do you not hear? And do you not remember?"* He was giving me everything I needed but I wasn't stopping long enough to hear, but as always, He will get our attention.

When I started laughing, I told Satan to get behind me, I was working for the Lord.

Our attitudes say so much about us and for me to have a good attitude; I must be a servant to others. Jesus washed the feet of His disciples at the last supper and cooked breakfast for them after His resurrection as stated in John 21:12, surely we can offer a kind word or hand to others. We should never be judgmental, because we don't know their circumstances, we just need to walk in the Light so they will see and want what we have. Sometimes, for no reason, bring someone a card, through inquiring and listening find out how they like their coffee, bring them a cup, in winter bring a flower, it's the little things that bring a smile to someone's face and oh, what pleasure we get from serving. Our goal everyday should be to put a smile on the face of someone and to help them understand the right attitude makes this journey called life easier.

Our prayer today: Dear God help us to always be good stewards and servants for Your glory. Ease the pain of the hurting and the sick, give them back their life and most of all Lord, thank you for loving us. Amen

Matthew 10:29-31, *"Are not two sparrows sold for a copper coin? And not one of them falls to the ground apart from your Father's will. But the very hairs of your head are all numbered. Do not fear therefore; you are of more value than many sparrows."*

Last evening I was sitting on my back porch watching the wind weave in and out of the tree branches while the leaves changed from dark to light green as they turned one way, then another. I had to laugh just a little; it was if they were holding on for dear life. I caught a mocking bird out of the corner of my eye trying to fly into the wind, ever see a bird suspended in mid-air? It's absolutely amazing to me.

The above scripture came to mind and I felt a blanket of peace cover me as I thought how much our Heavenly Father loves us. *"Yea though I walk through the valley"*, I fear not, no matter what our situation, He sees, knows and cares for us. Just as the leaves hold tight to the branches until their time to fall to earth, we should hold tight to the hand that can and will lead us through it all; our Savior. When we put our cares in God's hands, He puts His peace in our hearts.

We can find all kinds of encouragement in books, nature, family and songs. I especially love the words of this song; "I sing because I'm happy, I sing because I'm free. For His eye is on the sparrow, and I know His watches me." David C. McCasland. This song and these words will always lift me from my deepest depression.

If God sees the sparrow's fall,
Paints the lilies short and tall,
Gives the skies their azure hue,
Will He not then care for you? **Anonymous**

Our prayer today: Father, thank You for the wind, the trees, the birds, even down to the grass we walk on, I thank You for it as well. Everything I touch or see I know You put it here for our enjoyment. I feel so safe knowing You're watching over us every minute and I love You Father for loving me. I can't praise You enough. Amen.

Psalm 103: 15-17, *"As for man, his days are like grass; As a flower of the field, so he flourishes. For the wind passes over it, and it is gone, and its place remembers it no more. But the mercy of the Lord is from everlasting to everlasting on those who fear Him, and His righteousness to children's children."*

Philippians 2: 9-11, *"Therefore God also has highly exalted Him and given Him the name which is above every name, that at the name of Jesus every knee should bow, of those in heaven, and of those on earth, and of those under the earth, and that every tongue should confess that Jesus Christ is Lord, to the glory of God the Father."*

The first two weeks of June are normally the best time of year to visit our local mountains; so my sister and I decided to take a little trip. As our eyes were satisfied with the beauty of the native flowers and plants God put here for our amazement, we were also delighted as we watched the mountain creatures feasting on the flower nectar and berries. There were numerous bear, turkeys and deer.

Our actual mission wasn't to travel the Blue Ridge Parkway; we were destined for Murphy, North Carolina to visit a site called, Fields of The Wood. I had heard of this place and then pulled it up on the internet. Aren't computers great? You can travel the world and never leave your comfy chair. But leave your chair you

5

must if you want to download a memory you will take
to your grave.

As we drove in through a large white oval gate, I immediately felt the presence of God. Neither my sister
nor I said a word; we were in total awe at our surroundings. On one side of the mountain are the Ten Commandments. The letters and numerals, made out of
concrete, are four feet wide and five feet high. Above
this is the Bible which is 30 feet high and 50 feet wide,
quiet a sight. As we drove around this display to the
top of the mountain, we saw a cross made of flags representing every nation in the world. I thought about
the scripture John 11:52, *"and not for that nation only,
but also that He would gather together in one, the children of
God who were scattered abroad."* When you see this, it
quickly brings home just how small our world really is;
we all belong to Him.

We made our way back down the mountain and I noticed
a hole in the side of a hill with, what looked like a round
concrete slab, rolled halfway across the opening. As I
stood reading the sign which said this was a replica of
The Garden Tomb which was given by the state of Tennessee in 1944, I knew where I would be next. Before
I realized it, I had entered the room, and found myself
on my knees; not saying anything; God knew what was
in my heart and my thoughts. I don't remember ever

being where there was total silent, yet so much peace and warmth.

Our prayer today: Thank You Heavenly Father for paying the ultimate sacrifice for me. For loving me with all my faults. I pray, hold this round ball we call earth in Your tender hands and blow Your healing breath over it. Blow away all the disease and hatred, make us well again, Savior. I give You thanks and praise in the name of Your son Jesus. Amen.

I was on vacation last week and to my surprise, a much needed one. It's so easy to get in a rut and not even know it, sort of like ounces just before they turn into pounds, you didn't see them coming until they were there. My sister and I were in the mountains and I remarked to her to look at the clouds, I love the way it looks as though God takes His paint brush and makes little swirls. She said she never thought about looking at the clouds but now they would have a new meaning for her. As we rode along, I caught myself being absorbed by their every move and suddenly I reflected on, when was the last time I was lost in the clouds alone with God. Somewhere, somehow, I became to busy. Oh, I still took time every morning to read the Word....but that quiet time.....just Him and me was missing. You know God never asks us to be busy, He asks us to be joyful. So guess what a little time on your knees can accomplish, not only will it get you back on track but it will also give you that warm secure feeling only His love can provide.

Proverbs 17:22 says it best, *"A cheerful heart does good like medicine, but a broken spirit makes one sick."* God has made it crystal clear for a long healthy life we need to laugh and laugh a lot. I read this article recently which states, "recent studies have shown that laughter boosts the body's immune system, reduces stress, reduces the risk of heart attacks and even acts as a natural tranquilizer." So, now, every morning we should take a huge dose of our medicine called laughter prescribed by the great Physician. Lets keep Psalm 30:4 on our lips, *Sing praise to the Lord, you saints of His, and give thanks at the remembrance of His holy name*...now doesn't that put a jolt of joy in your soul? Jesus told us that we will face tribulations, but then He also says, "Take heart!" "When you have trouble, cheer up." What God is saying is that we can choose to be joyful and positive no matter what happens. He's already won our battle, whatever it may be.

Our prayer today: Lord, thank You for being my strength, I know all I have to do when trouble knocks is look up to You. Please show me how I can fulfill Your plan for me. Hold the sick and hurting close to Your bosom, so close Lord they will feel Your love and warmth. In Jesus' name....Amen

I came across a little story which I think puts into motion the very core of how rumors, gossip or untruths are started.

A certain little girl, when asked her name would reply, "I'm Mr. Sugarbrown's daughter." Her mother told her this was wrong, she must say, "I'm Jane Sugarbrown." The Vicar spoke to her in Sunday School and said, "aren't you Mr. Sugarbrown's daughter?" She replied, "I thought I was, but my mother says I'm not."

Guess who was standing too close and had to hear the conversation, Mrs. Telephone, telegraph, tell blabber mouth. Without knowing the truth, she seized the opportunity to put out an all points bulletin to her friends, this is how people's lives are changed, over a few misinterpreted words. Matthew 7:5 puts it this way, *"Hypocrite!. First remove the plank from your own eye, and then you will see clearly to remove the speck out of your brother's eye."* We need to ask ourselves why would I intentionally or unintentionally say anything that might hurt another. Do I think I'm better or I know more than they do? Am I promoting myself when actually I should be lifting this person up with what I think is their problem to God? These are some of the logs we need to remove from our own hearts. I don't honestly believe any of us have any malice for our neighbor, it just happens and don't we feel bad when it does? We must learn to be more like our Father...who tenderly keeps us close to His heart, our name is on His lips and watchfully, He never lets us out of His sight. I know we can, we are to cover each others back, being a safe harbor and an inspirational light. Maybe we can put a screen in our mouths to filter out the wrong words.

Our prayer today: Dear God, make me more like You so I can go about doing Your work and be the light someone needs today...heal the sick, hurting and desperate, I pray...Amen

This morning I pulled in front of my building and like every morning, I thanked God for delivering me safe, put my sun visor on the dash, grabbed my things, got out, locked the doors and as I looked toward Heaven, I saw a beautiful sight. There was one spot in the clouds with sun streaks peeking through and I thought of the pictures I have always seen of Angels looking down, reminding us, "you're safe, we're here." As I thanked Him for allowing me to see this I thought how awesome God really is. He puts us where we need to be at the right time and we think this just happens. He always comes through, not on our schedules but on the one that counts, He's never late. Sometimes I steal away to a place where I can reflect on my yesterdays and all I can do is praise Him for His mercy and grace. He has given me so many miracles, I can't keep count.

Psalm 37:4-5, *Delight yourself also in the Lord, and He shall give you the desires of your heart. Commit your way to the Lord, Trust also in Him and He shall bring it to pass. "* When God sees us giving praise at a dark moment, He says to the angels, "Look at that one. She's praising Me even though her doctor told her about the cancer. That man just lost his job, and yet he's praising Me. Hurry, angels, take healing and comfort to those and pour out blessings they cannot contain." Notice the order in which these things happen, He tells us not to fret, but to trust, delight and commit ourselves to Him. We need to bundle our burdens, give them to Him and praise Him for His blessings. He is waiting to pour out His blessings on us, if only we ask.

Our prayer today: Lord I do praise You in all things; You are so awesome and thank You for loving me. I do pray for the hurting and sick today, touch their hearts and bodies, heal them is my humble prayer and as You have given me the words to send once again today, thank You precious God. Amen.

Yesterday I was on the elevator with three ladies I didn't recognize as working in my building, which is fine in itself, but I noticed one looking down at the floor while the other two were involved in what looked like a twosome conversation. I have seen the time I would have stood and looked at the floor also not wanting anyone to acknowledge I was there, but not anymore.

I said to the lady, I haven't seen you before, extended my hand and told her my name. Her smile was kind and beautiful as she took my hand and told me hers. The elevator came to a stop; I thanked them for visiting our building and to please come back. In John 1: 4 & 5, *In Him was life, and the life was the light of men. And the light shines in the darkness and the darkness did not comprehend it."* As believers, we have come to know Him and have found that His will is love. As subjects of Christ, we are implored to do His will, which involves actively caring for others. This is how we , "Let our light shine" for Him. On this journey we call life, if we can remember one scripture, it should be John 10:10, *"The thief does not come except to steal, kill and to destroy. I have come that you may have life and have it more abundantly."* I think this says it all, the devil wants and will try to take everything we hold dear including our self confidence. If he can take this, then he has us beat down, we feel alone, unwanted, worthless. But then we remember, nothing can happen to us that looking up and reaching for His hand won't cure.

The next time you see someone needing a helping hand, reach yours out and extend God's love letting His light shine through you.

Our prayer today: God thank You for Your love, help us to remember we all need each other, this is how You made us. Please heal the sick and hurting as we pray in Christ' name...Amen

I don't how many of us love Bogangles chicken, but as for me and my family, we do. Tuesdays are my late night at work and I don't go home and start cooking. While I was standing in line last evening I noticed this well dressed, yet noticeably agitated woman, whose actions I thought might need observing. I must admit the line was long and I already figured I would be there roughly 15 minutes but that's to be expected sometimes. After noticing the expert customer service the young lady behind the counter was demonstrating I thought, Lord touch the heart of this woman and form her lips where nothing but kind words will come from her mouth. In Philippians 1:6, *He who has begun a good work in you will complete it until the day of Jesus Christ.* In other words God loves us enough to accept us as we are, but He loves us too much to leave us that way. Also let's read Proverbs 16:1, *The preparations of the heart belong to man, but the answer of the tongue is from the Lord.* Now since I have your curiosity, the woman gave her order, received her goods and quietly left. As I stood there feeling tension from the floor up, I lowered my head and said, Thank you God. I remember the saying you often hear during flight, landing is a crash under control. I think this was an altercation under control which is also good, after all, look who the Mediator was.

Every morning we should stand in front of our mirror and seek God's guidance, that we might be able to show love to our neighbors as He shows love to us. What

God thinks of us is more important than what we think of ourselves or the opinion of others, because we are saved by His mercy, not by our merit. Kind words don't cost anything, yet we reserve them for a special few. Use things and love people, don't use people and love things. Things can be replaced, the impression you leave in someone's heart stays.

Our prayer today: God, I know I can be a blessing to someone today. Open my eyes to all of the ways I can serve those around me with a cheerful heart. Heal the sick and hurting is my daily prayer, ease their pain. I want to shine for You today and do Thy will. In Jesus name...Amen

As I was driving in to work this morning, I witnessed a crash under control, in other words, it was a near collision. These two cars were beside each other and one started easing over the center line, the person in the opposite vehicle recognized what was happening and blew their horn which startled the first driver to take corrective measures. What happened next was typical, brake lights, windows came down, hand gestures and language not fit for any ears to hear, not even a sailors'. I could see the devil laughing and pointing at those two drivers, he was bursting his sides. I got to thinking he's pro-active which makes us re-active, he can get inside our head, but he can't get inside our heart, this is reserved for God only. Ephesians 4: 23, *and be renewed in the spirit of your mind.* One of the most important areas we need to clean out first is get rid of the negative, put in its place the positive. By thinking positive, we will speak positive and if we do this enough, one day we will realize things are so much better.

We can become pro-active by practicing self-discipline and I think this includes the five second rule. Before we answer a confrontational question we should take a deep breath, most of the time this gives our brain time to absorb the content and respond in a way that's pleasing to the receiver and to us. I know I have responded without thinking and later ask, "Father forgive me, I don't know why I said that, if I could just go back and change it", or, "the devil made me do it." But you know as scary as it is, it's true and he's sitting in a corner somewhere having a good laugh.   I thank my Savior, I've learned to be more pro-active so now when I "can't help myself" I have the last laugh and it feels good.   When you feel down and out, no one loves you, no one understands or cares, just remember John 10:10, *"The thief does not come except to steal, and to kill, and to destroy. I have come that they may have life, and that they may have it more abundantly."* Learn to say this verse everyday of your life.   We are bigger than the devil because God loves us, all we have to do is believe this and be happy, how hard is that?   We can start by doing a good body shake and find someone to be nice too, this will always make you feel better.

Our prayer today: Lord, help me to always remember no one can defeat me for I know You love me.   Everyday I feel Your arms holding me, keeping me safe and You will give me everything I need to continue this journey and make it to the end.   Precious Lord touch the sick and hurting, they so need You today.   Amen

Have you noticed, if we include the power of positive thinking and adopt a better attitude, most of the time it slides right on to the people around us? In today's busy and hectic society we don't think we have the time to show kindness. People are so wrapped up in their own little worlds, their focus is on I, Me and Mine. It's a sad situation when we spend eight hours a day, five days a week with each other and never even consider their needs. Sometimes we should stop and thank Him for giving us the ability to be here and the knowledge to practice His word in Matthew 22: 37-40 *"You shall love the Lord God with all your heart, with all your soul, and with all your mind. This is the first and greatest commandment. And the second is like it: You shall love your neighbor as yourself. On these two commandments hang all the Law and the Prophets."* We are here for a reason and this just might be to let one person see His Light through us. We need to use a good body peel and shed the person we have become by giving in to the demands of the world. We are all guilty of wanting to be like someone else, this drains us both mentally and physically. We unintentionally take our frustrations out on our families, co-workers and even ourselves. God has formed us the way He wants us to be and loves us unconditionally. Granted, it's hard sometimes to treat others with kindness and respect when we watch them lie, cheat and steal their way to the top of the corporate ladder, but life isn't really about getting what you deserve, life is what you make it. I think we should all stop for a moment and think about

God's word, it's not up for debate, we should take this very serious.

Matthew 7: 21, *Not everyone who says to Me, Lord, Lord, shall enter the kingdom of heaven, but he who does the will of My Father in heaven."* Being a Christian is not an organized religion, nor is it a certain denomination, it is a way of life and if you doubt this try putting on the armor of God and see what happens, talk about an attitude change, others will want to be like you . When we do this our negatives are gone and we start focusing on the positives. We can also start by saying thank you when our fellow employees help us, we can go out of our way to be kind, because, our co-workers are people too.

Our prayer today: Lord, I pray, use me for Your glory today, give me a word, gesture or expression so one will focus on You. May I always speak with a kind mouth and listen with a sympathetic ear. Lord, touch the sick and hurting today, we have so many feeling hopeless and helpless. We ask these things in the name of Your Son Jesus....Amen

Once again, this past Saturday, I was driving the Blue Ridge Parkway. You can't live in North Carolina and not visit the parkway this time of year, it's inhumane. I've learned the mountains are beautiful anytime. It doesn't matter what season they are in and at this time of year they're getting ready for a long rest. I've also noticed the people you meet have removed their tattered garments for one of pure joy. They glow with the ease of the moment, so relaxed and fulfilled. No one blows their horn at you or rides your bumper, their hand gestures are a sincere "hi." Isn't this great, God in all His splendor." People are not afraid to say His name because around every turn you see more of Him, His spirit pierces your heart and soul. We stopped at an overlook and when I stepped from the car I thought I heard a water fall but as I turned toward the mountain I saw it was the sound of the leaves hitting against each other as they fell to the ground. They were forming a beautiful tapestry to keep their roots warm and I thought of Joseph and his coat of many colors. At a time like this the Psalm 46:10 comes to mind, *"Be still, and know that I am God."* If you get the opportunity to see the changing of the leaves, notice people when they get out of their cars, perfect silence, everyone is feeling God's serene and perpetual presence. Peace on earth has never been more evident.

Imagine with me for a moment, God forming Adam and the look of love He must have had on His face as

He gave him two eyes, just maybe He might have said, "my child, these I give to you so you can see and appreciate the awesome beauty I have made for you." In Isaiah 42:6, *"I, the Lord, have called you in righteousness, and will hold your hand; I will keep you and give you as a covenant to the people."* I'm confident you feel the same as I do concerning this scripture, it gives me such joy and comfort to know, it doesn't matter how bad it gets, God is there to take our hand and lead us through it. Everyday, with no exceptions, we should bow our heads and declare, this "will" be the best day of my life and I'm going to be happy because I choose to, I "will" live each moment as if it's my last because it might be.

Our prayer today: Thank you Lord for allowing me the vision and the time to see all of Your awesome beauty...I pray Lord, touch the sick and hurting, they so need to know You are near. Comfort them and bathe them in Your tender mercy.....Amen

I don't how many of us love Bogangles chicken, but as for me and my family, we do. Tuesdays are my late night at work and I don't go home and start cooking. While I was standing in line last evening I noticed this well dressed, yet noticeably agitated woman, whose actions I thought might need observing. I must admit the line was long and I already figured I would be there roughly 15 minutes but that's to be expected sometimes. After noticing the expert customer service the young lady behind the counter was demonstrating I thought, Lord touch the heart of this woman and form her lips where nothing but kind words will come from her mouth. In Philippians 1:6, *"He who has begun a good work in you will complete it until the day of Jesus Christ."* In other words God loves us enough to accept us as we are, but He loves us too much to leave us that way. Also lets read Proverbs 16:1, *The preparations of the heart belong to man, but the answer of the tongue is from the Lord.* Now since I have your curiosity, the woman gave her order, received her goods and quietly left. As I stood there feeling tension from the floor up, I lowered my head and said, Thank you God. I remember the saying you often hear during flight, landing is a crash under control. I think this was an altercation under control which is also good, after all, look who the Mediator was.

Every morning we should stand in front of our mirror and seek God's guidance, that we might be able to show love to our neighbors as He shows love to us. What God thinks of us is more important than what we think of ourselves or the opinion of others, because we are saved by His mercy, not by our merit. Kind words don't cost anything, yet we reserve them for a special few. Use things and love people, don't use people and love things. Things can be replaced, the impression you leave in someone's heart stays.

Our prayer today: God, I know I can be a blessing to someone today. Open my eyes to all of the ways I can serve those around me with a cheerful heart. Heal the sick and hurting is my daily prayer, ease their pain. I want to shine for You today and do Thy will. In Jesus name...Amen

Proverbs 15:20, *"A wise son makes a father glad, But a foolish man despises his mother."*
Proverbs 22:6, *"Train up a child in the way he should go, And when he is old he will not depart from it."*

Once again, I overheard Dr. James Dobson making a statement concerning our children. He said their habits aren't taught, they are caught. Our children think everything we do is correct and they want to be just like us. If we could get inside their mind and eyes to see ourselves as we go through our daily lives, I wonder, would there be anything we'd change? Of course we would.

This had never been more evident than last Saturday. I was shopping for just the right card, in one of our buy everything with one stop department stores, when this family of four decided to look for a card to give to their mother and grandmother. I must truthfully say, never had I witnessed total disregard of respect or manners for each other. The father would push the girls away to get the card he was eyeing, and then they would yell at him "to stop it", he would yell back, "shut-up you little stupid brats." At this point the mother slapped the dad and both girls on their backsides of which those three retaliated by hitting her arms. I put my card back, went to my car, bowed my head and prayed. I wiped the tears from my face as I started my car; this song was playing on the radio. As I listened, I knew this was the message our Heavenly Father wanted delivered.

"Listen to the children while they play, ain't it **kinda funny** what the children say?"

"Daddy hates mamma, mamma hates dad, last night you should've heard the fight they had."

"Gave little sister another bad dream, woke us all up with a terrible scream."

"Cheat on your taxes don't be a fool, what was that they said about the golden rule?"

"Never mind the rules just play to win, hate your neighbor for the shade of his skin."

"Stab'em in the back that's the name of the game, and daddy and mama are the ones to blame."

"Listen to the children while they play, it's **not really funny** what the children say."

I have said so many times as I'm sure each of us have, oh God if only I could go back, I would do things differently. I would be more attentive to my family and the needs of those around me. The most wonderful thing is, we're still here and we still have time to help others. We can't start over but we can start correcting our mistakes by first realizing He left us here for a reason.

Our prayer today: Thank You Father for my loving children and I pray, protect the helpless ones of this world. Show me and lead me in the way I should go. I am Your servant, use me for Your glory. I ask in the name of Jesus. Amen

Matthew 20: 26-28, *"but whoever desires to become great among you, let him be your servant. And whoever desires to be first among you, let him be your slave, just as the Son of Man did not come to be served, but to serve and to give His life a ransom for many."*

Proverbs 3: 27-28, *"Do not withhold good from those to whom it is due, when it is in the power of your hand to do so. Do not say to your neighbor, "go and come back and tomorrow I will give it," when you have it with you."*

Like most, as I was getting dressed this morning, I had the local news on. I listened to a story about an eleven year old boy named Zachary, which caught my attention because this is my first grandson's name. This precious angel is walking from South Florida to Washington DC to draw attention to the minds of all of us, the needs of the ever increasing number of homeless children.

As I watched new houses being bulldozed in Nevada last month, I remarked to my brother and sister-in-law, "this upsets me beyond belief." Families sleeping tonight in the woods would gladly tear down those houses; carry the boards one by one off the developer's property, just to get the materials. We have boarded up buildings here in my town and the city council is talking about knocking them down. There again, all this material will be sent to our local landfills. *"Do not say to your neighbor, "go and come back tomorrow and I will give it, when you have it with you,"* came to my mind. We keep talking about and planning to provide for the homeless, when if we would

just stop thinking about it and open our eyes, we would
see we already have all the resources we need. What's
the saying? we can do great things for the Lord if we are
willing to do little things for others.

I think this is what Jesus had in mind in one of His last
conversations with His disciples. He wanted to show
them the full extent of His love. So before their last
meal together, He took off His outer garment, wrapped
a towel around His waist and began to wash their feet.
This was very shocking for them since this was a chore
performed by slaves only. This was an act of servant
hood and a symbol that pointed to Jesus' sacrifice, passion and humiliation on the cross. His request to His
disciples was: *"If I then, your Lord and Teacher, have washed
your feet, you also ought to wash one another's feet,* John 13:14.
They were to "pay it forward," and so are we.

Imagine how different our world would look if we gave
the kind of love to others that God has given us through
Jesus. To know love, open your heart to Jesus. To show
love, open your heart to others.

Our prayer today: Heavenly Father thank You for giving me all I have and need. Guide my steps and teach
me ways to help others. Bless the hearts and minds of
those who freely give of themselves everyday. This world
holds many who are hurting and feeling so alone, mostly
through no fault of their own, show us a way to help.
We ask this in the name of Your Son Jesus. Amen.

2 Corinthians 5:7 & 8, *"For we walk by faith, not by sight. We are confident, yes, well pleased rather to be absent from the body and to be present with the Lord."*

In our lives we come across many firsts. Our first day in school, first love, first car or house. Maybe the first time we pruned a rose bush or mowed the grass. Life is full of firsts and these are the ones we look back on with either fond or painful memories. When we lose someone we love or someone we deeply care for, we start a new round of firsts. First birthday without them, first Christmas and the list goes on.

This time last year we were celebrating my husband's birthday in Mayberry, North Carolina. He picked this town because as he put it, "this is how God intended things to be, quiet, unhurried and people who respect each other." The family gathered from New Jersey, Tennessee, Georgia and Florida. As we migrated to the large gazebo, we all held hands with no phones ringing, sirens blasting or televisions blaring, just a cool breeze taking all our troubles with it. We knew in our hearts this would be the last time we would celebrate his birthday here on earth. However, he got to live a life long dream of getting to ride in the patrol car used on the Andy Griffith show, driven by a man representing Goober. My husband was treated like a king as he waved to the people on the narrow streets, enjoying every minute of it, but as he later told me, he was looking forward to his next birthday, celebrating it with The King. What a gift.

I found a poem written by Henry van Dyke which I think sums up our passing from this world to the next. "I am standing at the seashore. A ship at my side spreads her white sails to the morning breeze and starts for the blue ocean. I stand and watch her until; at length, she hangs like a speck of white clouds, just where the sea and sky come to mingle with each other....And just at the moment when someone at my side says: "There, she is gone!" There are other eyes watching her coming, and other voices ready to take up the glad shout: "Here she comes!" And that is dying."

So, today as we start a new group of firsts, Psalm 23 comes to mind, *"Yea, though I walk through the valley of the shadow of death I will fear no evil."* Through means we aren't stopping, we're coming out the other side as safe as when we entered. Can't you just see the angels preparing a banquet and welcoming us with open arms when our Father decides it's time for us to come home....oh Father, I can only imagine.

Our prayer today: Father in Heaven, thank You for giving me a diligent spirit. Thank You for Your faithfulness. Give me strength to stand until I see Your promises fulfilled in my life. Help us to remember when we lose someone we love, with it comes a list of new firsts.

But we can get through this when we realize our loss becomes their gain. This void in our hearts will again one day be filled with upmost joy when we see Your face and our loved ones standing next to You. I ask and receive these things in the name of Jesus. Amen.

Matthews 21:29 *"He answered and said, I will not, but after-wards he regretted it and went."*

Have you ever faced an unwanted chore and felt as if it was the last thing on earth you wanted to do? Cleaning the house, mowing the lawn, paying bills or the worse one of all, admitting you're wrong and apologizing. This one can cause us, too much of the time, to procras-tinate. When this happens, I have a motto I repeat to myself, "I don't feel like it but I'm going to do it anyway." I know I'm going to feel better once I have completed my task, so why not just go ahead and get it behind me.

We all get in a hurry sometimes and forget what we're doing, how we sound to others or maybe the hurt we cause another. Here's two recent examples for me. After church Sunday I went to the cemetery and then stopped to fill my car; of course I had to go in and pay before pumping. The cashier was busy restocking shelves and finished the box she was trying to empty before coming to the front to take my money. She never said a word, just took my card and put it in the register. Already be-ing inconvenienced by having to wait, you can imagine how I must have sounded when I said "and good morn-ing to you." I walked back to my car and beat myself while the outdated pump slowly filled my tank. I had to smile, God was giving me the opportunity to think about my actions. When I went back inside to get my change, I said to her, "having to work on Sunday is a bummer,

you're a special person to do this for people like me."
She smiled and said, "Thanks, I need a job."

My brother came over last Saturday and caught me looking out the window. He said, what are you looking so
intense at? I have a split rail fence and two had broken,
which made a perfect "V" twenty feet apart, not a pretty
sight. I told him that fence was an eye sore and I keep
putting off replacing the rails, although it's eating me
alive. He opened the back door and said lets go. I really
didn't feel up to it, but I found myself at home depot
helping him load the truck. It took us longer to replace
the old ones than it did to go get them, but the fence
looks good again and my neighbors are happy. Another
job off my mind.

God is interested in our faith and obedience, not just
our good intentions. The next time we are tempted
to shirk our duties, why not say, "I don't feel like it,"
then ask God for the grace to do it anyway. We never
know who's watching or listening. We're leaving a
lasting impression, either good or bad. Lets choose
good.

Our prayer today: Heavenly Father today I submit my
dreams, desires and fears to You, I trust that You are
out for my good and I desire only Your plan for my life.
Confirm the plans You have for me so that I can walk in
Your ways. I pray in the name of Jesus. Amen

Ruth 1:16 *"Entreat me not to leave you, or to turn back from following after you; For wherever you go, I will go; Your people shall be my people, and your God, my God."*

As I learned yesterday, while having a conversation with co-workers, they're already setting up tent communities in California for the people who have been evicted from their homes due to the foreclosure boom. Being homeless is real, not having a job is real, not being able to feed your children is real, but Hebrews 13:5 keeps coming forth from the data base of my mind, *"I will never leave you, nor forsake you."* We all know this, however, sometimes we let go of everything we know to be fact. He's with us "all" the time, in our hour of need and our hour of plenty; He has something planned for our good.

I found this article and thought about how desperate these people must have felt. In May of 1989, a massive rainstorm filled Lake Conemaugh in Pennsylvania until the dam finally gave way. A wall of water 40 feet high traveling at 40 mph came rushing down the valley toward Johnstown. It picked up buildings, animals and human beings and sent them crashing down the spillway. When the lake had emptied itself, debris covered 30 acres and 2,209 people were dead.

At first, stunned by the loss of property and loved ones, survivors felt hopeless. But later, community leaders gave speeches about how local industry and homes could be rebuilt. Just this little positive approach acted like a healing balm and the survivors energetically got to work. Johnstown was rebuilt and today is a thriving town with a population of approximately 28,000.

We're all feeling a little apprehensive in today's world, and some have suffered great loss, but lets look at the resources and relationships that remain and trust God to use them. This can inspire the hope of rebuilding a new life in all of us. Lets speak positive over everything,

Our prayer today: Father God, thank You for Your faithfulness to me; for guiding and directing my steps. Help me each day to give "thought" to my ways and to follow the good plan You have for me. Continue the angelic wall around the helpless children and elderly of this world. Touch the sick and hurting; heal their every pain and unhealthy thought. We ask and receive these things in the name of Jesus. Amen.

Philippians 2:1-4, *"Therefore if there is any consolation in Christ, if any comfort of love, if any fellowship of the Spirit, if any affection and mercy, fulfill my joy by being like-minded, having the same love, being of one accord of one mind. Let nothing be done through selfish ambition or conceit, but in lowliness of mind let each esteem others better than himself. Let each of you look out not only for his own interests, but also for the interests of others.*

I fill in some Sundays at the Living Center for my church, getting the elderly ready and helping them down to the chapel. I had the pleasure of meeting a beautiful couple who shared a brief overview of their lives with me. They have been married for 76 years, he's 96 and she's 92. Do the math, he was 20 and she was 16. Could it be vows were taken more serious in those days? What caught my eye was the fact he was pushing her in the wheelchair and as he turned her around to face the pulpit, he kissed her on top of her head. Proverbs 18:22 came to mind, *"He who finds a wife finds a good thing and obtains favor from the Lord."* This was so evident just watching and listening to these two.

There was another couple; I learned they have been married for 43 years. He's stubborn and won't let her help him with his wheelchair, but this past Sunday I saw a side of him that was pure love. They got separated, people with wheelchairs and walkers were trying to get in line at the cafeteria, there she stood asking everyone that came by had they seen her husband. I pushed him right up to her, and when she realized it was her husband, she started crying and whispered, "I thought you were gone." He grabbed her hands, kissed them, smiled up at her and said "I wouldn't go anywhere without you." The scripture, *"fulfill my joy by being like-minded, having the same love, being of one accord of one mind"* certainly describes these two. I held her in my arms until she got herself together and then escorted them to lunch.

We are to treat each other in this same way. So many are hurting today, and if we can simply find in our hearts a kind word, a warm smile or helping hand, just imagine how far this can go. I think this is the reason God made more than one person; we need each other for comfort.

Our prayer today: Heavenly Father thank You for putting certain people in our lives to help us and others for us to help. I submit every area of my heart to You. Let everything I do or say bring glory to Your Precious Name. I ask this in the name of Jesus. Amen

1 Corinthians 2:9 & 12, *"But as it is written, Eye has not seen, nor ear heard, nor have entered into the heart of man the things which God has prepared for those who love him. Now we have received, not the spirit of the world, but the Spirit who is from God, that we might know the things that have been freely given to us by God."*

Psalm 23:4, *"Yea, though I walk through the valley of the shadow of death, I will fear no evil; For You are with me; Your rod and Your staff, they comfort me."*

Have you ever tried to imagine what God might have in store for your future? No matter how great the dreams are you have in your database, God has more in store for you. I hope you're like me, I'm like a little child, I get so excited when each new day begins..."Father, what plans do You have for me today."

A large number of us watch Biggest Loser and last night Mike finally was able to admit to himself and his dad the reason he had gained so much weight. Even as a child he would look at his dad and say, I'm never going to be that big. But we all know what happened; he did. Resentment is like a parasite; it feeds on us and leaves us weakened. It's only purpose is to take from and leave us with negative energy. It eats at the very core of our soul and robs our mind of any good feelings.

God is a creative god and His thoughts and plans go way beyond anything we could ever imagine. As the scripture says, "*He will lead you through it.*" The bible says we will have trials, but if we stay focused, God will lead us through anything. Did He say our lives would be as soft as a bed of roses? No, but He's always there for us to fall back on. Our strong pillar if you will. Mike's dream was and still is to become a doctor. He knew, with the weight he was carrying, he would never be taken seriously. I grant you if someone should ask him now if he had any idea he would, today, be on the Biggest Loser and have lost more weight than any man on the show before; he would probably laugh in your face. But God knew; isn't He something?

We all have dreams, as well we should, being hopeful is what gets us through the day. When we learn to open our eyes and actually see our Heavenly Father, things are going to be so much better. He's everywhere we look and everywhere we go, He's right beside us, so let's get our expectancy up. Let's start by focusing on what we have, not on what we're lacking. Stop fretting about what we should have been and concentrate on what could be. Today...this very day...let's forgive, forget and move on. Let go of resentment and you'll be amazed by all the space it leaves in your life for better things, the good things God wants us to have. Live each day with excitement. After all, today is all we have, we're not promised tomorrow.

Our prayer today: Heavenly Father, thank You for loving me and for preparing great things for my future. Help my thoughts to become agreeable to Your will. Increase my vision and give me Your strength to fulfill all that You have placed in my heart. Heal the sick and hurting; ease all their pain and suffering. Protect the helpless children and elderly of this world. I ask and receive these things in the name of Jesus. Amen

Ephesians 1:3, *"Blessed be the God and Father of our Lord Jesus Christ, who has blessed us with every spiritual blessing in the heavenly places in Christ."*
2 Corinthians 1:3, *"Blessed be the God and Father of our Lord Jesus Christ, the Father of mercies and God of all comfort."*
1 Peter 1:3, *Blessed be the God and Father of our Lord Jesus Christ, who according to His abundant mercy has begotten us again to a living hope through the resurrection of Jesus Christ from the dead.*

Being the mother of three boys, I recently came to the realization they all have their father's characteristics. Each one cares deeply for family, they love to work in their yards and it shows. You will never catch one without his pocket knife, truck keys, wallet and debit card. As I watched the habits of my number three son this passed weekend, I saw his dad in everything he did. He is now the proud father of two boys. If you ask them what they would like to be when they grow up, "just like my dad," will always be their answer. This brought to memory the words their grandfather would sometimes use, "little eyes are watching every move and listening to every word." "We must be careful, very careful, to always set the right example." This goes for mother's as well, our children think we are the know all, supply all and their protector at all times.

It's not unlike our privilege as God's children. At salvation we are placed "in Christ" and granted full access to all the valuable resources He offers us; resources such as His wisdom, forgiveness and grace. New perspectives that bring hope and confidence even in the toughest of times, material provision and peace are also ours in Him. God lavishes His resources on us "according to the riches of His grace." (Eps, 1:7) I know at the end of a long day, when I get home and have my quiet time with my Savior, everything is going to be alright. As with our children, He's my defender, counselor and supplier.

I found this little poem by Adams which I feel is a perfect fit today:
"I know not by what methods rare the Lord provides for me;
I only know that all my needs He meets so graciously."
We don't have to know the reasons for our God's love and provisions, we just need to accept them and be so thankful.

Our prayer today: Father in Heaven, thank You for making me a new creation. Thank You for empowering me to live as an over comer. I give this day to You and ask You to help me fully understand the plan You have for me. I ask these things in the name of Jesus. Amen

Acts 17: 27-30, *"so that they should seek the Lord, in the hope that they might grope for Him and find Him, though He is not far from each one of us; for in Him we live and move and have our being, as also some of your own poets have said, 'For we are also His offspring.' Therefore, since we are the offspring of God, we ought not to think that the Divine Nature is like gold or silver or stone, something shaped by art and man's devising. Truly, these times of ignorance God overlooked, but now commands all men everywhere to repent."*

How many times have we all played games with our children or remember playing them with our parents? We made a lot's of good memories didn't we? I read a story about a father and his boys playing a game called "sardines." He said when his boys were small, they would turn out all the lights in their home and he would hide in a closet or some other cramped place. The rest of the family groped about in the darkness to find his hiding place and then hide there with him until they all squeezed together like sardines.

His smallest family member at times would become frightened in the dark, so when he came close, he would whisper to him softly; "Here I am." "I found you, Dad!" we would announce as he snuggled against him in the darkness, not realizing his dad had allowed himself to be "found."

Likewise, we have been made to search for God, to "grope" for Him, as Paul put it so vividly in Acts. But here's the good news; He is not at all hard to find, for "He is not far from each one of us." He desires to make Himself known as He calls to us softly; "Here I am." When we get to feeling down and alone, look at the sky, the oceans, mountains, trees, He's everywhere watching over us. We know it when that calm, serene feeling covers our body.

Before we come to know Christ, we reach for Him in the darkness. But if we search for Him in earnest, He will make Himself known, for *"He rewards those who diligently seek Him."* Heb 11:6. *"We need to seek the Lord while He may be found, call upon Him while He is near."* Isaiah 55:6.

We all need the assurance or the bond with our Heavenly Father. What a sad place this would be if we couldn't talk to Him everyday.

Our prayer today: Thank You Father God for the comfort I feel everyday, just knowing You're close by. No one or anything can harm me as long as I call on Your name. We have many hurting today and feeling so alone, touch them Lord and whisper softly, "it's going to be alright, I'm in control." I ask and receive this in the name of Jesus. Amen.

Romans 1:20-21, *"For since the creation of the world His invisible attributes are clearly seen."*
Psalm 19: 1, *"The heavens declare the glory of God; And the firmament shows His handiwork."*

Last Saturday I went searching for a DMV office which I thought might be open, however, after leaving one, stopping to ask directions to where another one might be, only to find it closed as well, I thought, what a waste of my time and gas. Just then I went around a curve in Kannapolis, NC, I think it's called the loop, and I was immediately in another world. Psalm 23: 2 came to mind, *"He leads me beside the still waters. He restores my soul."* This was a picture perfect place, a retreat from the pressures of life. I forgot about my frustrations, took a deep breath and rested in the moment. I couldn't wait to call my sister-in-law, she said come get us. She took pictures of the endless cherry tree blossoms as I drove and this kept crossing my thought process, how very, very smart God is! He is the one who figured out how to make living things grow and they all grow according to a lot of very complicated rules that He put into every living thing. God's knowledge is vast. His wisdom is beyond our ability to understand and His beauty is shown in all of the flowers, butterflies, trees and mountains of our world.

We have all read the Book of Job and toward the end, God confronted Job and humbled this man who nearly accused God of doing what was wrong. God asked of Job, *"Where were you when I laid the foundation of the earth? Tell me, if you have the understanding. Who determined its measurements—surely you know! Or who stretched the line upon it? On what were its bases sunk, or who laid its cornerstone, when the morning stars sang together and all the sons of God shouted for joy? Or who shut in the sea with doors when it burst out from the womb, when I made clouds its garment and thick darkness its swaddling band, and prescribed limits for it and set bars and doors, and said, 'Thus far shall you come, and no farther, and here shall your proud waves be stayed'?"* (Job 38:4-11). Consider the greatness of the universe God made and how detailed and exact everything is that God has fashioned! We truly do learn much about God's greatness and glory just by noticing the world all around us.

Let's take just a little time and look for God today in everything we see. We all need retreats in our lives, not only because of the overwhelming nature of life, but because of our dependence on the resources of the Master. In our fast-paced days, it is essential to find a place of solitude, "a place of quiet rest, near to the heart of God." I enjoy the birds singing to me each morning as I leave for work and I'm always looking at the sky, searching the clouds; He could be on the next one I see.

Our Prayer today: Heavenly Father, thank You for Your faithfulness to me. Thank You for giving me strength

during the difficult times of my life. I trust that You are
with today and choose to focus on the victory You have
in store. I ask this in the name of Jesus. Amen

2 Samuel 9: 3, 6, 8, 11 *"Then the king said, "Is there not still someone of the house of Saul, to whom I may show the kindness of God?" And Ziba said to the king, "There is still a son of Jonathan who is lame in his feet." (6) Now when Mephibosbeth the son of Jonathan, the son of Saul, had come to David, he fell on his face. Then David said, "Mephibosbeth?" And he answered, "Here is your servant." (8) Then he bowed his head and said, "why would you look upon such a dead dog as I?" (11) Then Ziba said to the king, "According to all that my lord the king has commanded his servant, so will your servant do." "As for Mephibosbeth," said the king, "he shall eat at my table like one of the king's sons."*

I must confess, this morning I had every intention of writing about God's beauty concerning our blanket of white He placed over us Monday. The deer running across the fields at Philip Morris and the black washed fence posts with their little pointed caps, each pretty much the same, but I couldn't get this person and his family off my mind after reading this scripture.

Sometime ago I worked with a young man who, both he and his wife, became very dear to me. They had been married for several years and decided it was time to start a family. Jubilation quickly turned to horror as they were told; all indications showed their son had Down syndrome. They were sent home to think about aborting or, the nightmares they were to face. Knowing these two as I did, I knew what their decision would

be. He was born with Down syndrome but his parents
didn't see it at all. As that baby looked up at his parents,
all he saw was two pair of loving eyes that only saw pure
perfection.

As with Gene Stallings and his only son, Johnny, who
was born with Down Syndrome. He wasn't supposed to
live longer than five years, but he made it to forty-six.
He was his father's heart, his buddy as Gene would call
him. Jill Briscoe wrote a true story concerning a couple who prayed to God for a child and everyone made
fun of them. The baby was born with Down syndrome
and when the father went back to work he wondered
how he was going to face his co-workers. "God, please
give me wisdom," he prayed and just as he feared, some
mocked, "so God gave you this child!" The new father
stood for a long time, silently asking God for help, then
he said, "I'm glad the Lord gave this child to me and
not to you."

As this man accepted his disabled son as God's gift to
him, so David was pleased to show kindness to Jonathan's son, who was "lame in his feet." In God's eyes, every person is important. He sent His only Son to die for
us. This should remind us how much He values each
human life. Hug someone today, tell them they look
nice or simply smile, this goes a long way.

Our prayer today: Lord may we see in those we meet the imprint of You and may our love and care make them grow stronger. As Your creations, love is what makes us the person You intend for us to be. Father God, I thank You for loving me and I pray, give me the love in my heart each and every day to share with others I meet. I ask these things in the name of Your Son Jesus. Amen.

Revelation 3: 20-22 *"Behold, I stand at the door and knock. If anyone hears My voice and opens the door, I will come in to him and dine with him, and he with Me. (21) To him who overcomes I will grant to sit with Me on My throne, as I also overcame and sat down with My Father on His throne. (22) He who has an ear, let him hear what the Spirit says to the churches."*

If I asked the question, "Where's Waldo?" you might recall those popular children's picture books from the 1980's. I was a librarian many years ago, and I know I'm dating myself, but that little guy, with his red-and-white shirt and hat loved to hide in the pages amid a busy blur of images that made it nearly impossible to find him. How many times have you wanted to run away and hide from everyone and your problems? I can assure you I have. Actually sometimes, I feel as though I stand out like a neon sign, people laughing and pointing their fingers at me. But then I remember our Father God's words, *"Be still and know I am God."*

Thankfully, finding Jesus is a lot easier than finding Waldo. Jesus doesn't play hide and seek. He says, "Behold, I stand at the door and knock." We can find Him at the door of our heart, the core of our existence, waiting to come in. He doesn't just want to meet us every Sunday at church, or to be considered whenever we feel ourselves coming unraveled. Rather, He longs to be in the center of our dreams, thoughts and desires.

In other words He wants a real relationship with the real you.

As wonderful as this is, we could find this to be a little unsettling sometimes. Our heart is no doubt harboring a few things He will want to deal with. But I also know there is nothing more valuable than intimacy with Him. Welcome Jesus in and He will clear out the clutter until the air is fragrant and fresh with the purity, power and pleasure of His presence. When I allow God to come in and deal with the mess I have made, I feel so much better. I even see the world differently; it looks prettier and I can see the beauty He put here for me. Welcome Him in and see what He can do for you, "He's knocking."

Our prayer today: Thank you Father for the blood of Jesus that cleanses me and helps me. Lord, I hope to always choose to follow the path of your Righteousness. May the door to my heart always be open to You. Please remind Your angels to maintain the wall around our children and elderly, the helpless ones of this world. I ask these things in the name of Jesus. Amen

Jeremiah 29:11, *"For I know the thoughts that I think toward you, says the Lord, thoughts of peace and not of evil, to give you a future and hope."*

Deuteronomy 30:9, *"The Lord your God will make you abound in all the work of your hands, in the fruit of your body, in the increase of your livestock, and in the produce of your land for good. For the Lord will again rejoice over you for good as He rejoiced over your father."*

Matthew 7, 27 & 28, 31 & 32, *"Which of you by worrying can add one cubit to his stature? So why do you worry about clothing? Consider the lilies of the field, how they grow; they neither toil nor spin; Therefore do not worry saying, what shall we eat? or what shall we drink? or what shall we wear? For after all these we seek, your Heavenly Father knows your need of all things."*

Today of all days, please read and absorb the above scriptures. We truly have nothing to worry about, it's already been taken care of for us. If the news media scored points for putting everyone, this includes the world, on edge, they wouldn't be able to count them all. Do I think they do this on purpose, of course not, they're just like us, they have families, homes and jobs they're concerned about; But again, lets put this all in perspective, it's happened before and we're still here, we still have a roof over our heads, food in the pantries and our children, who just by their smile, take all our stress away.

I took special notice of the clouds this morning as I drove in. The different shades of blue outlined by soft hues of pink was a soothing sight, and I thought to myself, Father, thank You for loving us, for giving us eyes to see all the beauty you put here to ease our fears and stress, this is better than yoga. I caught myself smiling as I felt the peace and energy filling my body. By this I knew we were all going to have a productive day. As I entered the building preparing for work, everyone I met had a big smile and I said, "yep, You're already here putting Your children at ease."

Let us remember, everything here on this earth, including us, is His. We own nothing, nor would have anything if He didn't want us to. So when we start to worry about the condition this world is in, knowing worrying won't get us anywhere, look up and around you, He's here taking care of the little things.

As in Revelation 3:8, *"I know all the things you do, and I have opened a door for you that no one can close. You have little strength. yet you obeyed my word and did not deny me."* I believe the door has already been opened and we're going to be alright.

Our prayer today: Heavenly Father, I thank You for using me as Your messenger all these years and I trust You will continue to do so. Hold everyone close so they will feel Your presence and know You're there waiting to ease their every fear. Continue to bless and heal the sick and shut-ins in hospitals. Have Your angelic army keep the wall of protection up for the elderly and children. I ask and receive these things in the name of Jesus. Amen

Philippians 4: 8-9, *"Finally, brethren, whatever things are true, whatever things are noble, whatever things are just, whatever things are pure, whatever things are lovely, whatever things are of good report, if there is any virtue and if there is anything praiseworthy-mediate on these thing."*

Ephesians 6: 1-4, *"Children obey your parents in the Lord, for this is right. Honor your father and mother, which is the first commandment with promise; that it may be well with you and you may live long on the earth. And you fathers, do not provoke your children to wrath, but bring them up in the training and admonition of the Lord."*

According to one little boy, "Thinking is when your mouth stays shut and your head keeps talking to itself." The way our head talks to itself tells a lot about how we are doing morally and spiritually.

My # 3 son was telling me about my grandson's football team losing their first game. To say the least he's a perfectionist and so very hard on himself. If you can envision this picture, and we all have seen this either by children or the pros, he takes off his helmet and prepares to throw it, just in time to hear his dad say, "you best not." This brings me to another time when this same dad was a small lad, same temper and demeanor. He decided to take out a glass door with a die-cast John Deere tractor because his older brother wouldn't give him back his car. When his dad got home, he looked at the door for a while, then turned to our son, "did you do this?" "Yes sir," was barely audible through his tearful voice. His dad's next question was, "well what do you think we should do about this?" And of course being a chip off the old block, he looked up at him and said, "I think a spanking." Of course his dad couldn't spank him, all he wanted to do was pick him up and hug him; he was noticeably moved by his honestly and strength. So he told him, no I think you should sit on the sofa, look at that broken glass and ask yourself, did I really have to do this. This is pretty much what our son said to his son, when you give your best that's all anyone can ask; dad is so proud of you. Hold your head up and know there will be another time.

Children do not learn to love and obey God only by what we say. They also learn by watching what we do. Along with what we say, we need to set an example by our love and obedience to our Father.

We can't be perfect parents, but our children must see our desire to please our Heavenly Father. And when we fall short, they need to see our repentance. We teach them both by what we say and what we do. Spoiled children are given what they want; wise parents give them what they need. When we see our youth acting out distastefully, maybe we need to look a little closer, just maybe it's us and just maybe we could try a little harder.

Our prayer today: Heavenly Father thank You for the gifts of my children, I know You love them even more than me. Hold me accountable for their conduct and upbringing, Help me to dwell on what is good and pure. May Your words control my every thought. May I learn to think with my mouth shut. Guard our young with Your mighty hand and love. I ask and receive these things in the name of Jesus. Amen

1 Timothy 6:6, "*Now godliness with contentment is great gain.*"

Hebrews 13:5, "*Let your conduct be without covetousness, and be content with such things as you have. For He Himself has said, "I will never leave you nor forsake you.*"

I have often been encouraged by people without their realizing it. I remember walking through the main lounge of a retirement home where my mother resided until God took her home, one evening. It was getting dusk and most of the residents had already gone to their rooms, except for one elderly woman. Unaware I was watching her; she patiently worked on a jigsaw puzzle with the most pleasant smile on her face. Maybe she was recalling her life, preparing meals for her family, helping her daughter get dressed for the prom or maybe she could feel the cool breeze across her face as she sat with her husband on a porch swing long ago.

I began to wonder; some people can find true contentment no matter what their circumstances. The apostle Paul addressed this in 1 Timothy. He warned against corrupt people who see godliness as a means for financial profits. A more common error among Christians is the belief that godliness plus money is life's winning combination. If you read the words Paul wrote, he corrected both these errors by saying; a real winning combination, "*Godliness with contentment is great gain.*" God will give us the desires of our heart as long as it is in line with His. True contentment is not in having everything, but in being satisfied with everything you have.

When we're young, most of the time we never think about eternity; we're going to live forever. We work, plan and put away for our golden years. Then one day it dawns on us, I had better start thinking about retirement; we've stood still but time marched right on by.

Isn't it comforting to know the angels haven't been idle; they have been busy preparing our final move. You see one day we're going to receive a retirement package that's out of this world and I am, like you, looking so forward to it. We will have fought the good fight and won.

Our prayer today: Heavenly Father I pray let my light so shine that others will seek You also. Help me keep my mind focused on the prize and keep persevering toward it. My wish and plan is to never steer one of Your children wrong. I pray hold the sick and hurting close and breathe Your healing breath over them. Protect the children and elderly of this world, keep them safe from all harm. I ask these things and receive them in the name of Jesus. Amen

Hebrews 13:5 & 15, *Let your conduct be without covetousness and be content with such things as you have. For He Himself has said, "I will never leave you nor forsake you." "Therefore by Him, let us continually offer the sacrifice of praise to God, that is, the fruit of our lips, giving thanks to His name."*

I thought of these scriptures Tuesday morning as I was leaving my home making my way to work. There in front of me was a picture that demanded my undivided attention. Immediately I knew Who it was and what this represented. I wanted to call everyone and say, "look to the East, you won't believe your eyes." But then at 6:30am, I also knew I wanted to keep these people as my family and friends. A white cloud was outlined with pinkish orange and at the bottom was a dark blue circle. From this there were three perfectly straight lines, one at 10:00 o'clock, 12:00 o'clock and 2:00 o'clock. I remember having this big smile on my face as I looked at each line and whispered, the Father, the Son and the Holy Spirit. Just at that moment Psalm 46:10, *"be still and know that I am God"* absolutely took over my thought process. I guess I would have been late for work, but the horn on the car behind me quickly brought me back to reality.

In these desperate, trying times we're living in, not knowing from day to the next about our future, I find this gives me more quality time to spend with my Heavenly Father. Time to thank Him for all He has given me,

I don't dwell on what I don't have, because apparently I don't need anything more. We have always heard and still do, "I don't know how they can afford all they have, one of these days I'll show'um." This is wrong thinking, God wants us to have the desires of our heart, but most of the time, our desires are only "stuff." No amount of stuff will ever make us happy. It's what's inside that counts, it's how we align our heart with our actions. I remember having a discussion with a friend not too long ago concerning finances and hardships. I asked him if he gave God His part, he said there's not any left for tithing. I reminded him tithing is one of God's laws and you're never going to get ahead by breaking it. If you lose your drivers license by speeding and you keep getting caught, guess what, you will never get it back; however, with our Heavenly Father it's different. If we give him his ten percent, He tells us in Luke 6:38, He'll give it back pressed down, shaken together and running over. God doesn't need our money, or anything of monetary value we have; it already belongs to Him, everything, absolutely everything is His; we own nothing nor can we lay claim to anything...except His love.

The next time you back out of your garage or driveway, stop and look for a second at your home and your surroundings, thank God for the roof over your head and ask His security for the ones left inside. Thank Him for the trees and grass that filters the air we'll breathe today. Put God first in everything you do and see if your life doesn't get better and better. One thing we should always keep stored in our data base is, we're preparing for a lifetime with Him. He made my feet so they could walk on streets of solid gold. It doesn't matter if on this beautiful earth my feet are deformed or if I'm in a wheel chair; I know one day I will stand and see my reflection smiling back at me. Just keep this is mind, we're going to leave everything we have labored day and night to acquire one of these days, so lets keep our priorities in order.

Our prayer today: Dear Father, I humbly come before you today and ask that You search the deepest places of my heart. Show me if there is any area where I need to line up my heart with my actions. Help me to be a shining light for You, use me for Your glory. May I always have a kind word of encouragement for others to hold on too. Father, please ease the suffering of the sick and hurting, clear the hospital beds. I ask these things in the name of Jesus. Amen.

Hebrews 12:1 & 2, *"Therefore, we also, since we are sur-rounded by so great a cloud of witnesses, let us lay aside every weight, and the sin which so easily ensnares us, and let us run with endurance the race that is set before us, looking unto Jesus, the author and finisher of our faith, who for the joy that was set before Him, endured the cross, despising the shame, and has sat down at the right hand of the throne of God. "*

You may have heard the story of John Stephen Akhwari, he was the runner from Tanzania at the 1968 Olympics in Mexico City who came in dead last. When we say dead last, this means never had anyone finished so far behind everyone else.

He was injured trying to get there, and with his leg bloodied and bandaged, he hobbled into the stadium. Most of the spectators were gone by the time he had crossed the finish line. When ask why he ran despite his pain, his reply was, "my country did not send me to Mexico City to start the race, they sent me to finish."

This same attitude I have seen in my Uncle L.B. Davis. He recently celebrated his 90th birthday with a small gathering at his son's home. In the center of the ta-ble was a cake proudly topped with a John Deere trac-tor. He had farmed the land his father and brothers all tended, never once stopping to think this was too much for one person. The shear vastness of the land made him thankful to God everyday for the opportunity and the strength to oversee and maintain this property, which as he had said many times, never belonged to him, I'm just the caretaker. Even at 90 years young, he never faltered, never asked for help. He knew his mission in life was to follow and obey his Heavenly Father and to leave the land as he found it for the next generation.

But now the John Deere tractors are all under their respective shelters and the land lays still. The final realization of a past lifestyle happened recently as he watched five loaded cattle trucks etch their way from his fields and drive past. In as little as five hours, a life he had known was vanishing in a trail of Georgia dust. I feel certain he looked up and said, "I know this is not the end for me, because I am still running the race and I won't stop until I see Your face." No one is ever too old to serve God and he's a perfect example. Although L.B. Davis and John Akhwari are from different worlds, they still have the same destination and are both looking forward to the day our Father says, "well done, good and faithful servant."

Our prayer today: Father, help me to always have a positive attitude about anything and everything. I know nothing is going to happen to me that You can't handle and already have the solution worked out. May I always keep my eye on the prize and never quit until I see Your face. I ask and receive these things in the name of Jesus. Amen.

Habakkuk 3:17 & 18, *Though the fig trees do not bud and there are no grapes on the vines, though the olive crop fails and the fields produce no food, though there are no sheep in the pen and no cattle in the stalls, yet I will rejoice in the Lord, I will be joyful in God my Savior."*

Have you noticed lately the nice cool mornings we're having? There's a fresh, crisp feel in the air. We start, with great anticipation, looking forward to the Master's breathtaking artwork as He dots the landscape with His brilliant colors of fall. This year as you take in all of His splendor, watch others around you. Most people say very little; they just look in childlike wonder, their eyes searching in amazement every detail. Some smile, others simply lower their heads in prayer. I saw a sign at a little country church not too long ago which read, "when you "bow" before God, you can "stand" before anything." I thought to myself how true, when we put God first, just look at how he removes the blinders from our eyes. We can walk in confidence knowing we're protected by His angelic army and we can see the beauty He put here for us more vividly.

Today as I listen to those around me, the same words are repeated over and over, people are so worried. Tune in to CNN or any news channel, all you hear is things are getting worse. In reading the above scripture I thought, this is evident of our lives today. Habakkuk's world was also coming apart at the seams, but he knew what to do when things seemed hopeless. And for some of us, our lives are literally falling apart because we think we have the fix all, cure all answers, what we need to do is as the prophet did, He rejoiced and praised the Lord in spite of everything.

We've all lost something or someone who was very dear to us and maybe we wanted to question or even blame God. Instead let's thank Him, not because we're suffering, but because we know He is still faithful and loving. God wants to bless us and lift us up above all our hurt and problems. He will see us through any obstacle to the other side.

Today let's turn a new leaf and start each day expecting God's best for us. When we open our eyes in the morning, before coffee, our shower or brushing our teeth, let's say "Thank You God for allowing me to see another day, and dear Lord, I'm eager to see what you have in store for me today." When you meet people, have a smile on your face and a little more bounce in your step. You can be certain someone will ask you why you're so happy, that's your perfect opportunity to say, I'm expecting something great today, aren't you? If we make this a habit, life will be so much better.

Our prayer today: God, bless us today with Your favor and Your love. I pray out loud those blessings on my friends and my family and believe they will happen. I believe in Your word and Your promise. Lord I need Your strength to stand up in the midst of troubled times and I thank You in spite of what is happening around me. I ask and receive these things in the name of Jesus. Amen

Psalm 4:1 *"Hear me when I call, O God of my righteousness! You have relieved me when I was in distress; have mercy on me and hear my prayer."*
Psalm 5:1-3 *"Give ear to my words, O Lord, consider my mediation, give heed to the voice of my cry, my King and my God, for to You I will pray. My voice You shall hear in the morning, O Lord; In the morning I will direct it to You, and I will look up.*

This morning when I got up, I quickly realized I was just as tired as when I went to bed. I know we all have mornings like this, and the first thing that crosses our mind is, this is going to be a long day. As I forced myself to get dressed, I made my way back to the kitchen for another cup of caffeine, hoping to get kick started and then, as I do every morning, I looked out the window and there He was. The white and blue clouds with their pinkest to light purple outline demanded my attention and quickly took my breath away. A sense of relief came over me as I accepted the fact... everything is going to okay in my world today.

Our God is a god of "suddenlies!" He can suddenly break an addiction. He can suddenly heal our body. He can suddenly open the door for that promotion we've been seeking. When we keep our heart expectant and filled with faith, it gives God something to work with. We all know Jesus turned the five loaves of bread and two fish into lunch for 5,000 men, Matthew 14:17, He will take our faith and turn it into the provisions we need.

I'm convinced the enemy lays awake at night thinking and planning of ways to steal our joy and get us down so we will give up and settle for less than God's best. As written in John 10:10, He came that we might have life and have it more abundantly.

I've learned, no matter how many disappointments or trials I face, God can turn it all around in a split second. One touch of His goodness can solve any problem we're facing today. Our Heavenly Father wants us to tell Him all about our troubles, although He already knows. It lets Him know we're taking Him at His word and trusting Him to follow through.

God didn't give us the talent to forget, He kept that for Himself, so we go through the motion of giving our problems to Him, but they're still stored in our data base. Oh, what a blessing it would be if we could forget and would stop trying to do His work for Him. When my plate gets to the point of running over, I just close my eyes and say, "Heavenly Father I need a hug from You." If you've never tried this, I pray you do.

Our prayer today: Dear God, each day I come before You with my joys, my problems, my praises and my requests. Please help to me learn to patiently wait with expectancy for Your answer, knowing Your plan supersedes anything I could ever hope to come up with. I ask and accept these things in the name of Jesus. Amen

Psalm 103:8, *"The Lord is merciful and gracious, slow to anger, and abounding in mercy."*
Lamentations 3:22-23, *"Through the Lord's mercies we are not consumed, Because His compassions fail not. They are new every morning; great is Your faithfulness."*
Romans 8:32, *"He who did not spare His own Son, but delivered Him up for us all, how shall He not with Him also freely give us all things?"*

As I drove in this morning I saw a lady standing beside her car, tire flat and cell phone ever present in hand. I had to smile as I thought back to the good old days when three men would have already pulled over to change it and a woman didn't have to be afraid. Lets all think back before computers, fax machines, answering machines, cell phones and pagers. Simpler times, before road rage and internet highways. Blissful times, when Sunday dinner was almost as special as the church service. When you took leisure walks or just had chats with a friend. When finding pictures in the clouds kept you happy by day and stargazing beneath a luminous sky soothed your soul at night. A time when a cool breeze would engulf your body and the first words out of your mouth was, "thank You God."

Sitting on the ice-cream freezer while a little bit of heaven on earth was being cranked out meant you were important to a very special event...family time. We always had a house full of relatives every Sunday. The moms and dads sitting outside laughing and talking while us kids climbed trees, swung on vines which hanged over the creek or played hide & seek. Those were the days when graciousness was as natural as breathing and people defined their lives by its meaning: grace, politeness, courtesy, kindness, respect and friendliness.

By remembering yesterday's simple joys and extending a cup of old-fashioned graciousness to others, you help keep the spirit of the good old days alive forever. Someone once said, "People may not remember what you did or said, but they'll remember how you made them feel."

So despite the world's condition, each time you bake some, just because I wanted too, cookies or cut a bouquet of beautiful summer flowers from your garden, bring some to a neighbor and let them know they're special. You'll keep the light of yesteryear burning by placing a memory in someone's mind. Isn't this how God lived and aren't we suppose to be like Him? Matthew 5:16 reads *"Let your light so shine before men, that they may see your good works and glorify your Father in heaven."* You never know how, what you do or say might affect another so we should always have on our shield of God's armor.

Our prayer today: Thank You, God, for the blessings you have given me. I can sit here and think of so many ways You have enriched my life. Give me an attitude of gratitude and I pray to always let Your light go before me. I ask and receive these things in the name of Jesus. Amen

Proverbs 2:6 - 8, *"For the Lord gives wisdom; from His mouth comes knowledge and understanding; He stores up sound wisdom for the upright; He is a shield to those who walk uprightly; He guards the paths of justice."*

When I woke up as a child we lived in Florida although I was born in Georgia.. I'm sure if you think back, the very first thing you can remember is what I call waking up. Living in Florida one can easily become complacent concerning hurricanes and tornadoes after all, it's the lightening capital of the world and we're still here. What's there to fear but fear itself, right?

As with most months during the summer, we were alerted to a hurricane just off shore that was coming across the panhandle of Florida. And as with all the years I had lived there and nothing happened, I brushed this warning off to the side of my thought process. I prepared my grocery list and my #3 son said "Mom I don't think I would buy anything that needs refrigeration, this one is going to hit us." I thought to myself, I lived through more of these warnings than he had and I'm not about to get excited about this one. I went on with my day, bought the groceries, put meats and frozen foods in the freezer and started to prepare dinner when to my surprise the winds begin to howl, the skies turned as night and the lightening was everywhere. Just at that time my husband and son came through the back door, I turned off the stove, we went to the den and sat in utter silence. All you could hear were trees breaking and the lightening cracking. Then everything went dark and we didn't have power for seven days.

As I watched that beautiful moon last night etch its way higher and higher, I thought of our God and all the things and warnings He has put here for us. He left us a guide to get through this race and how to set our eyes on the big prize. If we read His word and listen for His voice, I'm convinced we'll be alright. It brought to mind when I asked my son how he knew that hurricane was going to hit us, he said nature, just by it's actions you can always know what kind of day you're going to have. He said there wasn't a bird flying, no squirrels scurrying and the wind was deathly still. I wonder, have we stopped to notice the warnings before us this very day. God by His Word has said, "keep your eyes on Me and listen for My direction." Lets start looking and expecting Him to show us the way. We are His children and we should trust Him with every aspect of our days.

Our Prayer today: God, I confess I often turn to friends, talk shows and books for help before I think to seek Divine intervention. Please help me to ascertain the answers I am looking for right now. Grant me the wisdom and the understanding to tackle what I am facing today. I ask and accept these things in the name of Jesus. Amen

Genesis 8:22, *"While the earth remains, seedtime and harvest, and cold and heat, and winter and summer, and day and night shall not cease."*

As most of you know, my family and I are mountain lovers, so ever time we have the opportunity, we enjoy our. This past Saturday the trip was a little different, while we're driving down Hwy 441, which is six lanes I might add, I caught a glimpse of a patrol car as we went past each other. I saw him immediately slide over into the median and I said to my husband, he's going to pull me. He ask, how fast were you going? I told him 70, that's only five miles per hour over the speed limit, maybe it won't be too bad.

The officer followed us for about three miles and I had slowed to 65, and just when I thought I was home free, here came the blue lights. You see I quickly learned, as I passed a speed limit sign, I should have been going 55. I got my license out and handed it to him when he approached the car. His first question was, "What's your hurry Mrs. Elrod?" I guess I could have replied, I didn't realize the speed limit was 65, but I had no control over my monitor mouth, it was speaking actually what was on the hard drive of my heart. I just looked at his badge and asked, Trooper Hawkins have you ever really looked at these mountains? I looked at my husband as if to say, where did that come from? He said, ma'am I was born and raised here, but no, I don't guess I have.

I asked, couldn't he just see God down on one knee scooping out the dirt to form the oceans and with every handful He was creating a Masterpiece. Did He make them all the same, no, they are different heights and widths. There's a certain peace you feel when you're here, knowing you're looking into the face of God. Our Heavenly Father is in the business of making His children happy, that's the reason we look, point and say, look over there or look at this, we stay in total amazement and awe.

He gave me back my license and told me to slow it down. He would like to meet us again when we were in town, but not like this. Then as he walked back to his car, I noticed in my side mirror he was looking around at the scenery. As we pulled off my husband said, he's leaning against his car looking at the mountains.

I took the liberty of looking up the Macon County Highway Patrol of North Carolina on the intranet Monday when I came to work. I called and guess who answered the phone...Trooper Hawkins. He shared with me how the mountains have changed, from simply being there to things of awesome beauty, strength and peace. He said, " I now look for God everywhere and you know what...I see Him." He said he bought a Gaithers' CD and listens to it in his patrol car. I believe God puts us where we need to be to witness for Him, this was my time of seed.

Our prayer today: Father in Heaven, thank You for seedtime and harvest. Thank you for putting us where we need to be to share Your Word and love. Show me where to give the seed I have in my heart so that I can reap the harvest You have prepared for me. Amen.

Genesis 1:31, *Then God saw everything that He had made, and indeed it was very good.* 2:1, *Thus the heavens and the earth, and all the host of them, were finished.*

I had the opportunity to spend a couple of days at the cabin in the Smokey Mountains and although some would say, the mountains aren't pretty this time of year, to me they're absolutely breathtaking anytime. When I see the trees void of their leaves, it reminds me, everything has a season. This is the season of rest for them and quickly becoming a time of rejuvenation. As in the fall when God has taken His mighty hands and splattered the forest with brilliant colors, so it is now. All across the valleys and vast mountain sides, the leaves are ever so slightly pushing through and there's muted shades of reds, browns and greens everywhere. So, it is with us, we too have many seasons. From a season of being a helpless child to adulthood, then hopefully, enjoying ones golden years.

I want to share with you, if I can find the words, a sight God allowed me to see and I know it was for me since there wasn't another car on the parkway. The mountain incline was such that before I knew it I had climbed over 6000ft. The fog was settling and it was as if I was sitting in a plane looking out over the clouds. Large continuous bundles of different forms and every so often there would be a mountain peak protruding through. A deer ran across the road.... just one... and it was as if He said,

"My child here is another gift for you." The silence was beautiful and restful as I stood at the mountain's side and praised our Heavenly Father for giving me my eyes. As I prayed I thought of each of you and every person He had ever made, how I wish everyone could have been standing in my shoes and witnessing Gods handy work.

As each of us approach a new season of our lives, what makes it special is our attitude and what we bring with us, whether as an adolescent or senior citizen. We can bring years of loving service and character building for our Father or years of unbelief and defiantness. As in John 10:10, *He came that we might have life and have it more abundantly.* Just as we want the best for our families, so our Savior does for us. The next time something takes your breath away, thank the Creator. It didn't just happen, it was planned with great care and we're so very special to Him.

Our prayer today: Thank You Heavenly Father for claiming me as Your own, for giving all this beauty for my eyes to behold. Lord how I pray, keep my feet firmly planted on Your solid ground as I walk with You daily. Hold the sick and hurting close and ease their pain, build a secure wall around our children and elderly, keeping them safe from all harm. I pray these things in the name of Jesus. Amen

Revelation 5:9 & 10, *And they sang a new song, saying: "You are worthy to take the scroll, and to open its seals; For you were slain, And have redeemed us to God by Your blood. Out of every tribe and tongue and people and nation, And have made us kings and priests to our God; And we shall reign on the earth."*

This morning I was telling a dear friend in our break room about a majestic mural God had painted yesterday and as I picked up my cell phone to call my husband, he was calling me. I will describe what we saw and my prayer is, you saw it also. It looked like a contemporary painting one would see in the finest of mansions. There was a wide line of dark clouds, a clear opening of about the same distance, and then another line of dark clouds, but what made this so interesting was a perfect vertical wide line and evenly spaced from it was another perfect vertical line, just not as wide. The morning sun was shining on them and what a sight. All I could say was "thank You heavenly Father for allowing my eyes to see this; no one can paint like You"

This reminds me of an article I read sometime ago concerning a congregation who was planning to build a new sanctuary. Of course they wanted the absolute best, for they considered this was their way of showing God how much they worshipped Him. The center piece would be a stained glass window of children worshiping Jesus, so they hired the best artist their money could afford. He worked constantly without ceasing until he had finished what he thought was his masterpiece. That night he heard a noise, got out of bed and went to investigate. He saw a stranger altering his picture. "Stop!, Stop!, you'll ruin it," he shouted, but the stranger turned and answered, "you have already ruined it." The intruder explained all the children's faces were one color and he liked all colors. When the intruder said he wanted children of all races and nations to come to him, the artist stood in awe; he realized he was talking to Jesus Himself.

As the scripture says, He is worthy because of His shed blood and we all belong to Him. As Christians we are to work for unity and peace. Jesus went to the cross to bring salvation to people of every nation. Our witness must go beyond the barriers that have historically divided the human family. In this holiday time of year, with the economy as it is, I realize no one has a lot of money to spend on others, but lets remember the reason for the season, God gave His all. Children don't put price tags on gifts, they just want that special surprise all wrapped in pretty paper waiting for their little hands to rip open. Have you ever noticed the look of awe and total anticipation on the face of a child in the malls at Christmas? This is how we should approach everyday..."what surprise do You have for me today Father?"

Our prayer today: Thank You Lord for my eyes to see Your beauty everywhere I look. Instill in me the constant awareness of those around me, some You put there for me to help, others, You put there to help me. Father, my prayer this very day is, no child in any nation or any color will go unnoticed this most special of all holidays and that Christians will pray for and pursue everlasting peace for this part of Your universe we call home. I pray in the name of Your son Jesus. Amen

Psalm 46: 1 and 10, *God is our refuge and strength, a very present help in trouble.* *(10) Be still, and know that I am God; I will be exalted among the nations, I will be exalted in the earth.*

As I was driving in this morning, I was mesmerized by a very dark rim of clouds, shaped like mountains, lying just below a beautiful sapphire sky. Each one formed its own shape and peaks, I felt as though I was on the blue ridge parkway. *Be still and know that I am God,* kept playing in my mind, and what an awesome God He is. Everywhere we look, there He is, in the enormous sky, majestic trees, sprawling grasses, even the interstates.

Some people place their trust in wealth, but money cannot buy happiness. Some people trust knowledge, but the smartest minds cannot agree on the simplest of things. Some trust our military for protection, but there is no perfect peace. Some trust the company they work for to provide long-term security, but there is no such security. *God is our refuge and strength.* When we search for answers, He will provide them. When we need a shelter, He will provide it. When we need protection, His angels are there to surround us. The believer has *a very present help in trouble.* When we feel as though life is falling on top of us, we need to run to God's refuge. Inside we will find safety, security and love in His shelter that will survive any storm.

I would like to share with you something that happened to me recently. My husband was taken to the emergency room with heart failure. While I was leaning against a wall in his room praying, I saw two angels standing on the other side of his bed. For those of us who have seen angels, I know you will agree with me, there is no way to describe the material of their gowns. I am a seamstress and never have I seen this type of cloth in a store. The shade of white will not be found the in finest of mansions nor will it ever be duplicated by man. A peace of undefined words came over me and all I could say was, Heavenly Father I do see Your angels and this can only mean one of two things, You are taking him home or they're here to instruct the physicians, either way, Thy will be done. If you take him, I thank You for the years we've had and our wonderful sons, if he's to get well, I know You're waiting for him to fulfill his dream of feeding the deer along the stream beds in the mountains.

Our prayer today: Thank You Father for the feeling of security and peace You give each day. I feel Your presence everywhere I go and I so thank You for loving me. My deepest prayer today is for everyone to share Your calmness and find that place of refuge we all seek so desperately. Hold the sick and hurting close and blow Your healing breath over them. Protect the elderly and the helpless children of this world from all abuse. We accept and claim Your favor in the name of Jesus. Amen

Genesis 1:29, *And God said, "see I have given you every herb that yields seed which is on the face of all the earth, and every tree whose fruit yields seed; to you it shall be for food. "* Genesis 2:10, 15, *"Now a river went out of Eden to water the garden, and from there it parted and became four riverheads. "*
"Then the Lord God took the man and put him in the garden of Eden to tend and keep it. "

Earth Day is a beautiful reminder that God gave us this incredible gift and we're to preserve it with all our strength. Naturally though, as we share our planet with so many others, we run the risk of seeing it's beauty diminished and it's resources depleted. It breaks my heart, as I know it does yours, to see the rain forests being swept from the face of the earth and the oceans being polluted with everything we can throw in it. I've also noticed, if there's a piece of land with beautiful trees but no building, well let's take a bulldozer, get rid of all God put there and replace it with a concrete structure, when we have acres and acres of asphalt with abandoned buildings adorned with broken windows and gang graffiti. This is not exactly what I think God intended.

While we have every right to use the resources God placed in and on this earth, we also need to recognize our responsibility to respect it as His and to preserve it for future generations. In Genesis, the Lord told Adam to "tend and keep" the earth. Because we don't know when Jesus will return, we need to practice good stewardship, to leave our children and grandchildren some of the same resources we have learned to take for granted.

One way we can testify of our love for our Heavenly Father and to express our gratitude for what He has done is by tending and keeping the earth for all who follow. After all, we don't even own the grains of sand under our feet, it's all His.

D. De Haan wrote, **"The natural world that God has made is given to us and must be shared; may generations yet to come be thankful that we cared."**

Our prayer today: Thank You Heavenly Father for all the beauty You put here for my eyes to see, for all the sounds You put here for my ears to hear. May I never grow so cold as not to appreciate these daily and to let You know. Help me to do my best and my part to leave things here for others to admire and be in full awe of. Hold the sick and hurting close and breathe Your healing breath over them. Have Your angels build a fence around the children and elderly of this world and protect them. I ask this and receive it in the name of Jesus. Amen

Luke 8:39 *"return to your own house and tell what great things God has done for you. "* Psalm 24:1 *"The earth is the Lord's and all it's fullness, the world and those who dwell therein.*

Along with a large number of my family members, I stepped back in time this past weekend as we celebrated my husband's 76th birthday in Mayberry, North Carolina. This was the place he picked and, if I can recall his exact words, "I'm tired of the rat race, let's go someplace quiet where I can see the mountains." As the family gathered from New Jersey, Tennessee, Georgia and Florida, with hugs and laughter all around, we quickly migrated to the extra large gazebo where some played spinner or cards and some just held hands and talked.

As I watched their relaxing attitudes take place, I thought how wonderful this is, no phones ringing, no television or sirens blasting, just a nice cool breeze coming through the gazebo taking everyone's troubles with it. Then my number two grandson, who is three, came running, put his little arms around my neck and whispered, "I love you grandma." This moment I will take to my grave, but I thought, how many times our Heavenly Father whispers "I love you" to us. With every flower we admire, with every color that takes our breath away or the serenity we feel as He draws us close, that's love. Everywhere we look or anywhere we are, there He is; all we need to do is open our eyes and heart to appreciate His grandeur.

This earth is a beautiful creation of our Lord and "we the people" are forgetting His promise to us. *"Yea though I walk through the valley of the shadow of death I will fear no evil"*, Psalm 23. Through, means we aren't stopping, we're coming out the other side as safe as when we entered. This also reminds me, when we all started going back to our out of state residence, I was sad to see each one leave, but, on the other end, someone was happy they were coming home. Can't you just see the angels preparing a banquet and welcoming us with open arms when our Father decides it's time for us to come home. I'm sure we all feel the same way... I can only imagine.

Our prayer today: Thank You Heavenly Father for allowing me to see all your splendor and wonderment put here just for Your children to see. Thank You for the fellowship spent with my family and the new people I had the pleasure of meeting this weekend. I ask this and receive it in the name of Jesus. Amen

Galatians 6:9, *"And let us not grow weary while doing good, for in due season we shall reap if we don't lose heart."*

Most of you already know how much I love the mountains, this is where I feel closest to God. I was describing to my brother this past weekend, while on the parkway around Franklin, how I thought the mountains were formed. I can vividly see His huge, majestic figure down on one knee scooping the ground, creating holes, making way for the seas. And as He piles the dirt, I don't see Him turning to look at the height of each mound, for if you look at the mountains, they're all different sizes and shapes. He was a busy Father making a wonderful playground for His children to enjoy. I also noticed this is the season for slow down. Every living thing our Master created has a season. In the spring everything, including ourselves, is using stored energy from our restful winter to start anew. Then we are full steam ahead during the summer. If you notice in the fall we all start to slow down, taking deep breaths, absorbing everything around us, becoming more content, if you will, knowing our time of rest is at hand. The same for nature; the trees and plants are trying desperately to give us our last glimpse of God's greatness, then they will rest under their blanket of many colors.

God has a due season in store for us also. The Bible doesn't say you might reap, it says "you shall reap", if you don't give up. In order to reach our due season or harvest of blessing, we must continue to believe God's Word and confess His promises daily. We are the only one who knows what God has placed in our heart, and the evidence of that is what comes out of our mouth. Our word is our testimony and it shows where we stand. So often the only time we utter His name is when we're in dire need, but God wants us to count on Him twenty-four seven. He's always there and has a blessing for us we can't even imagine and it will come "if" we stay the course. Lets start today practicing saying His name, and use the one you like best, see how easy it will soon become a habit. I think God smiles when He hears us saying His sweet name.

Our Prayer today: God, this is the time for me to stand strong in my faith. Whatever the circumstances, I will confess Your power and mercy all the days of my life. I know You have a plan for me. Dear Father, please give me the patience to wait with a cheerful heart for my "season of blessing." Let my steadfastness be a light for others to see and want. I pray dear Lord in the name of Your son Jesus. Amen

Isaiah 58: 6-9 "*Is this not the fast that I have chosen; To loose the bonds of wickedness, To undo the heavy burdens, To let the oppressed go free, And that you break every yoke? Is it not to share your bread with the hungry, And that you bring to your house the poor who are cast out; When you see the naked, that you cover him, And not hide yourself from your own flesh? Then your light shall break forth like the morning, Your healing shall spring forth speedily, And your righteousness shall go before you; The glory of the Lord shall be your rear guard. Then you shall call, and the Lord will answer; You shall cry, and He will say, 'Here I am.' "*

Could He tell us anything we would enjoy hearing more than "here I am?" We can see Him everywhere we look, He's in the clouds, trees, mountains, the seas, and He's the air keeping the fowl of the skies soaring. Our God is awesome and yet I wonder just how much greater He would be to us if only we would change our way of thinking and our morals. I was coming home this past weekend from a family reunion and had listened to the radio for over one hundred miles telling me how the rich and famous live. When the DJ said this one lady's monthly mortgage payment was $50000, I had to pull over, I'm sorry, but the tears were flowing. I thought how we made these people rich and we have become so uncaring, we can't get enough of their perverse way of living. I wonder is it because we want to have a taste of how it would feel or does it keep us from facing reality? I looked at my husband and asked him, how many children and homeless do you think are out there in those woods? How many children and elderly will go to sleep hungry tonight? We have closed our eyes or so long, most of us are blind.

I took a brief survey today to find out what was the one thing people would like to see changed in America. The first was put prayer back in schools. then eliminate drugs and the dealers, followed closely by, getting a grip on violence, next came racism and then the illegal alien issue. Now lets look at how we can make this all happen, and some would argue with us, it's impossible, can't be done, we're too far gone. I'm a firm believer. nothing is impossible with God. I read recently where it cost $80,000 a year, (yes a year) to house one inmate, the cost for that same person going to a local university is just over $8,000. Now since it's our money paying the prison system, I want to see a change. Why can't the ones who would like to further their education go to college, just maybe we could reduce the prison population. Just maybe if we put prayer back in schools a lot of our problems would be solved. After all the Ten Commandments aren't multiple choice and our young need to learn this. As His Word says, when we do His will, then He'll send healing to our world.

Our prayer today: Dear God, thank You for allowing me to see another day, place in my heart a caring attitude and give me the strength to make change possible for Your beautiful world. Father, we give You thanks in the name of Your son Jesus. Amen

John 16:13, *"But , when He, the Spirit of Truth, has come, He will take your hand and guide you into all the truth there is. "*

I know today's preferred mode of fast transportation is flying, and let me go on record as stating, while I have flown, and yes I do know flying is safer than driving, I still prefer taking my chances on the ground. I remember the last time I flew I naturally had to have the window seat and as I looked down I could see the winding paths of the rivers below. Except for some man-made waterways, all rivers have one thing in common...they are all crooked. The reason is simple...they follow the path of least resistance. They will find their way around anything that blocks their paths, somewhat like humans. We fail to resist the devil because it's easier to yield to temptation and deviate from the path God wants us to follow.

God wants to help us make the right decisions. He's there to warn us when we're about to make a mistake, or about to get into areas that are questionable and may bring us harm. If we would think of our conscience as an alarm clock we would realize, He's that nervous feeling we get, that uneasiness we hear telling us what we're about to do is not in our best interest. This Holy Spirit feeling is not in your head, it's in your heart and you can learn to hear His voice. The more time you spend with God, really getting to know Him, the more you will be able to discern His voice guiding and directing you.

When I think about certain things that didn't happen to or for me, I find my quiet corner with my Father and as I start dissecting the events, I find a pattern of God winks, things I didn't understand at the time but suddenly becomes very clear.

One particular evening I was tired and decided we would have chicken for dinner, of course the deli was out and wasn't going to cook anymore, okay I thought, plan B. I'll order a slab of ribs, all out, okay...I've never had to go to plan C, so let's see what's next. I'll buy a can of clam chowder and I'll cook grilled cheese sandwiches. As I put my foot on the top step going into the kitchen I heard a terrible noise. The cable on the garage door broke with such force that it came down the passenger side of the car and through the wall into the laundry room. Had the deli personnel been on their numbers, I would have been getting the food out of the car at that very moment. As I surveyed the damage, all I could think of was, "Thank You God." Looking back I have to smile as I think about all the moves He went through keeping me from straying off path. Isn't our Lord awesome? Maybe we could all take a few minutes out of our busy schedules and thank Him for His guidance and for keeping us on the right path.

Our Prayer today: God, when I spend time with You, I grow closer to You and learn to listen for Your voice. Thank You for giving me Your Spirit that I may grow wiser. Help me to always look for the straight path and to remember it's a mistake to think I can impress the world by compromising with it. Give the ones who have a lost a loved one this week the peace they so desperately need. I ask this in the name of Your son Jesus. Amen

I watched a little boy trying desperately to get his mother's attention Sunday as she was attempting to tie his shoe...He kept saying "I can do it mykeft, I can do it mykeft." Finally she said okay, he smiled so big just knowing he was going to show her how much he had learned, but what he hadn't realized was his legs were too short to reach the floor from his chair. So as he leaned further and further over, he fell and bumped his head on the back of the chair in front of them. His mom, looking so concerned, ask if it hurt, "no", he said but I could see the defiant, stubborn little attitude boys are known for coming through. I have lived this scene many, many times having three boys of my own. We push our children to learn and to be independent knowing one day they will have to fend for themselves. This is pretty much the same way God treats us, He lets us bump our head sometimes to teach us to follow Him, not the flesh.

Ephesians 2:4, 5 &10, " *But God, who is rich in mercy, because of His great love with which He loved us, even when we were dead in trespasses, made us alive together with Christ. For we are His workmanship, created in Christ Jesus for good works, which God prepared beforehand that we should walk in them.* " God knows what we're thinking and what we're going to do before we do it, but as the scripture puts it, from His mercy and love we can't escape. This is a good thing, because no matter how difficult life becomes or how low others make us feel, all we have to do is "stop" take His hand, put on the shield of faith, hold our head up and walk right through any obstacle. I, like some of you, have bumped my head many times, actually had bruises on my body and scars on heart, but when I learned my Savior could take all of this away and make me a new person, my life has never been the same. I can now walk with confidence knowing He loves me unconditionally. Is the flesh going to surface ever so often? Yes. Is He going to let me suffer just a little? Yes. This will remind me to follow His lead and will. We can't run away from ourselves, or ourkeft, but we can put our lives in the hands of our Father.

Our prayer today: Father, thank You for your promises and blessings, thank You for loving us, thank You for always being there for us, just as our earthly father, You are our heavenly Father. Hold the sick and hurting close and ease their suffering and pain. Lord, my heart goes out to the children of this world, have Your angels put their wings around and over each of them and protect them from harm and pain. Clothe, feed and blow Your loving breath over them I pray. I ask this in the name of Your son Jesus...Amen and Amen.

Psalm 46:1 *God is our refuge and strength, an ever-present help in trouble.* Psalm 150: 6 & 7, *Let everything that has breath praise the Lord. Praise the Lord!*

Have you noticed the nights are getting a little cooler? And did you notice the bright, full, perfectly round moon this morning, doesn't it just give you hope? As the Psalmist said, Lets all praise the Lord, for we know the heat wave will soon be over, and I'm praising Him even now for rain, for this too will come.

I had to go and put gas in my car last evening, and there's this certain route I can take which normally has deer grazing. The past two times I didn't see any... too hot I think, but this time, as I was approaching the fields, I silently prayed, Precious Lord please let me see a deer, tonight of all nights I need to feel Your presence, I not only saw a deer, I saw a little herd. I got so excited I nearly left the road which wouldn't have been a good thing. All I could say was, thank you Lord for allowing me to see just a fragment of Your mighty works. This brings me back to the scripture, God is our refuge and strength. Not sometimes, but everyday most of us will face trials, temptations, hurt and pain. That's part of life and His word tells us we'll go through adversity, but we need to focus on what is really important. If we truly trust God, we know this will pass. Lets try looking at the things He has given us simply for our pleasure, like for me the deer.

I was struck with the beauty of the moon this morning as I was driving in, I caught myself saying, Lord, You made that moon, Your son Jesus walked under it with His disciples and I'm riding along here looking at it, is this not awesome, Praise Your name. The next time you find yourself really appreciating something He put on this earth, put it in your memory bank so when trouble seeks you out, and we all know it will, you can pull up your archive file and focus on it. You'll be surprised how quickly your sorrow is replaced with gratefulness and praise. When we remember everyone has problems, and we program ourselves not be robbed of our God given right to joy and peace, this journey we call life will go smoother.

Our prayer today: Thank You God for all the beauty You put here for our eyes and fulfillment, beauty to ease our sorrows and give us peace. Help us to always look for the good in everything and to always say something positive after every negative word that comes from our mouths. We ask these things in the name of Your son Jesus. Amen

Today I need to start with refreshing scriptures as in Psalm 51:12 *"Restore to me the joy of Your salvation, and uphold me with Your generous Spirit,"* and then in Psalm 55:22, *" Cast your burden on the Lord, and He shall never permit the righteous to be moved."* These words came to me at 5:00a.m., this morning as I stood in coffee on my kitchen floor. Not only was it puddled on the floor, the rugs were soaked, my once white drawer fronts were now antique white and while trying to clean them I had to remove everything from the drawers which also had coffee. But I learned two new things, it's okay to laugh at yourself and I absolutely hate mopping before I've had at least two cups of coffee and my shower. Since I refuse to let the devil steal my joy, I cleaned up everything, prepared a fresh pot of coffee and started singing Love lifted Me. Then it suddenly dawned on me, when was the last time I actually heard an adult laugh at themselves. When you're young the worst thing that can happen is to be ridiculed by others, the embarrassment of being laughed at and, God forbid, you would make fun of yourself, it just didn't happen. But as we grow older we learn laughing at ourselves is okay, it's also fun. Laughing puts things in perspective and chases away embarrassment, so, the next time you do something for which you feel remorse or things don't go your way, laugh at yourself and see how good it feels.

Life is too short for us to be up tight all the time and another thought that comes to mind, is no matter how hard we try, we will never own anything, God is the rightful owner of our possessions and we'll leave them behind when we shed this earthly suit for one of pure perfection, what an absolute thought. We need to give up ownership rights and take our stewardship responsibilities seriously. This does not mean adopting a casual, wasteful attitude about material things, but appreciating what our Lord has entrusted to us. If we can remember this, we will then take better care of things and enjoy life, knowing we're just passing through and what we leave behind is what people will remember us by.

God owns the gold in every mine.
The cattle on the hills.
And in His sovereign grace He gives
According as He wills. D. De Haan

Our prayer today: Dear God thank You for allowing us to hold and see all the beauty You put here for us, for as Your children, we see things through a different pair of eyes than others. We see You and the love You put in everything. We know You will always be here to protect us. We pray, pull the sick and hurting close to Your bosom and ease their pain. We ask this in the name of Your son Jesus....Amen and Amen.

I listened to an author promote his new book called God Winks and I had to put a lot of thought and energy into this making sense for me, but when you stop and analyze certain situations, God wasn't just smiling on you, He had His eyes on you, that means He put out His powerful hand and nudged you in the right direction. Can't you see this, Him turning and guiding us like a shepherd with his sheep, putting us where we need to be. Joshua 1:9 tells us *"Have I not commanded you? Be strong and of good courage; do not be afraid nor be dismayed, for the Lord your God is with you wherever you go."* Every time I think about this scripture, I feel closer to my Savior as I'm sure you do. Monday I was driving in to work, when suddenly I realized I was talking to God, telling Him how pretty the trees and flowers were this time of year and thanking Him for putting them here for our enjoyment. I could actually feel Him in front of my car, I just smiled and whispered thank You Lord..... thank You Lord. That made my day complete although it was just getting started.

Our responsibilities and challenges of life can steal our joy if we're not careful and this is when we need to stop and focus on what's really important. God has always used nature to snatch me back to His way of thinking. He uses nature to paint a larger picture than our lives, this gives us a broader focus. The Master Artist wants us to find His meaning in the painting He has created just for us. Look and see, observe and think, take delight in the little things that often go unnoticed in our hurried schedules. God wants us to Praise Him, to thank Him for all He has done for us and each new day brings new blessings. We are to bask in the fragrance of His heavenly bounty, the breeze the angel's wings produce and the beauty His brush strokes make. When you actually stop and see all of the wonders He makes daily just for you, this is a God wink.

Our prayer today : Oh, dear God, thank You for the beauty my eyes see everyday and Your blessings....use me Lord to pour out these same blessings to others who need to know You. I praise You in the name of Your son Jesus. Amen

Have you noticed spring is here, the different shades of green leaves pushing the fragrant flowers from their delicate vases which delight so many of us? Some will produce fruit while others will make a beautiful shade we can use to retreat from the sun. The Bradford pear trees look like one giant white egg, then they start to drop their petals and you would think it was snowing. Here's this thin white blanket covering their little feet and time has come full circle, just a few months earlier, they had a blanket of many colors to keep them from freezing. If you get the opportunity, look down into a tulip, absolutely amazing. Listen to the birds fluttering about, singing their peaceful tunes, we must wonder, how does He do all of this. I don't think ours is to wonder but more to enjoy and marvel at just how great He is.

In John 14:14, 15 & 18, *"If you ask any thing in my name, I will do it. If you love me, keep my commandments. I will not leave you comfortless; I will come to you."* God has given us Power of Attorney over all of His creations, we're to protect, admire and appreciate everything He's put here for our benefit. The scripture *"I will not leave you comfortless; I will come to you,"* is evident everywhere you look. He is telling us, "I'm here, relax, feel my presence." I wish I could have you close your eyes and listen to me tell you all the places God is. When you feel a slight breeze cover your body, that's God, when you smell the salty sea air, that's God, when hear the cry of a baby, the singing of the birds, that's God, when you look at the brush strokes of different colors forming the clouds, that's Him also. His comfort is everywhere we are, no matter if we're at work, shopping or at home with our families, He's there. God wants His children to be happy and secure in knowing of His love. So today we need to turn a new leaf and be proactive not reactive to the devil. We should say to him, "come on, make my day, are you ready to take on my Redeemer? I am so tired of seeing how the devil destroys lives, through our families, friends and work place. It breaks my heart when I see someone with their head down in despair but then I remember His promise and I can see hope for the future of this person...you see the devil beats us and beat us, until he beats us down to our knees; this is right where God wants us. From our knees we can look up and get up because our Protector is taking care of the problem. Every time you start to think about a past sin of which you know our Lord had forgiven you or a fear of a dreaded disease begins to creep back in to your memory, say devil get behind me for I'm marching forward with my God.

Our prayer today: God, thank You for giving me what You know I need everyday. Help me to recognize the struggles I go through is a way of growing in You and they will make me stronger. Hold the sick and hurting close to Your bosom as we ask this in the name of Jesus... Amen and Amen.

I'm sure we all have a favorite place at our home where we seek God in the quiet of the morning and mine is the small windows above the large ones in my living room. They're about ten inches high and 26 inches wide, I don't know their name, I'm not an architect, but they face the East and I can watch as the dawn breaks. The clouds are still a dark gray and some form together to make different shapes and I always thank Him for my eyes, the vision to see this. I often pray for the ones who have never seen the beauty He puts here daily for our enjoyment, but then how do I know they can't see, they may see more than we do. God is so awesome, I don't believe He made all of this for a select few.

Matthew 9:29 says, *"Because of your faith it will happen"*, I take this to heart. I fully believe whatever we ask in the name of Jesus will be done, but first we must have the faith. We should never say," God if You think I'm worthy", or "if You think one of these days You might have a minute for me." God wants the very best for us, as the scripture says, *"I knew you before I formed you in your mother's womb"*. To God we're precious and beautiful, we're His children and He loves us unconditionally. All we have to do is ask in faith knowing it will be done, maybe not on our time table, and in our way of thinking He's not coming through, but He is, He's never late, He knows our needs before we even ask. Let's start each day expecting something good from our Lord.

Our prayer today: God help us to remember Your word, "where there is no vision, the people perish." We ask Your help in praying with faith, with the certainty that when we ask in the name of Your Son Jesus, we should know without a doubt it will be done. Amen.

Dawning

D id you know our Heavenly Father performed a miracle out of His love for you and me. First He came as a little child, then paid the ultimate price, He died on a cross, but just as He had promised, on the third day He rose from the grave. During these three days, the earth shook twice, once when He gave up His spirit and the second when the Angel of the Lord descended from Heaven. Matthew 27:45-53 tells of this death and resurrection, *"Now from the sixth hour* (12 noon) *there was darkness over all the land unto the ninth hour* (3pm). The Expositor study Bible reads, for these three hours, God would literally hide His Face from His Son; during this time, Jesus did bear the sin penalty for all mankind.

We need to think about our sins, fornication, pride, gossip, hate, lying, indifference, unfaithfulness, rebellion and the list could go on. It was in this dark hour that God put our sin upon Christ. He bore the iniquity of us all, all of us being then and now. As He was being beaten, mocked and spit upon in Luke 23:34 we read He said, *"Father forgive them for they know not what they do."* He could have easily removed Himself from the cross, He could have wiped out the Roman army, He could have annihilated everyone around Him, but His love was too strong. Each person there heard His last cry, *Father, into Thy hands I commend my Spirit,"* and *"It is finished."* The Lord by the power of His own will yielded up His Spirit and died. The earth shook, rocks split and the saints rose from their graves, everyone stood frozen in utter horror. The Roman centurion standing close by got the picture. At the close of this event he proclaimed, "truly, this was the Son of God, certainly this man was innocent."

The Chief Priests and Pharisees remembered Jesus saying He would rise in three days and thinking the disciples would steal His body during the night, they asked Pilate for permission to fortify the tomb. They tied a cord, or rope, around the stone that covered the entrance and then sealed it with wax or it could have been clay, so that if anyone did try to take the body, the seal would be broken, therefore proving He didn't rise from the dead. Then four guards constantly stood in front. But just before dawn of the third day, these brave soldiers with all their armor and training as written in Matthew 28:4 *"and for fear of Him* (the Angel) *did shake and became as dead men."* This is the second time the earth shook, the Angel of the Lord descended from

Heaven and rolled back the stone, took a seat on top of it and said, "see He has risen." I don't know about you, but this gives me such joy, I'm actually laughing on the inside as I write this...in my mind I can see those brave little souls lying on the ground in a begging stance. This should remind us there's nothing, absolutely nothing our God can't do and when we ask Him to come live in us, we can move mountains or better yet, we can tell the mountain to move and it's done. All we need is the faith of a mustard seed, think for a moment how small that would be. If we believe in Him with all our heart, nothing is impossible for us through Him.

Our prayer today: God, thank You for saving me from my sins, the ultimate price was paid so I could live knowing one day I'll be with You. Please help me to let go of my old ways and totally put You in charge of my relationships, finances and my life. Again, thank You for sending Your precious Son to take my place. Amen

Lamentations 3:25, *"The Lord is good to those who wait for Him, to the soul who seeks Him."*
Psalms, 139:23-24, *"Search me, O God, and know my heart; Try me, and know my anxieties; And see if there is any wicked way in me, and lead me in the way everlasting."*

Yesterday I was conversing with a dear friend in Roanoke, Virginia and she was telling me how she watched the sun come up over the mountains Easter morning as she attended sunrise service. Some mountains had dark shades of green while others were a bright light green; it all depended on the direction of the sun's rays. Dawn is a special time of day, everything is renewed and we're fresh, no problems, no horns blowing or angry words being spoken, we're all at peace.

This brought to mind something I will always remember. Several years ago on an Easter morning, I had gotten up at 6. I opened the door to our porch to spend some quiet time before waking my husband for our sunrise worship. It sounded as though there were a thousand birds singing. I just stood in awe for a moment lost in the magical noise, not wanting to move but realizing I had to share this. I hurriedly, but quietly, made my way back in, woke my husband and asked him to please come listen. To my great joy, as we stepped back outside, they were still singing. He listened for awhile then whispered, "have you ever heard anything like this, they know He has risen. Our wonderful Savior is the creator of all things."

"The Lord is good to those who seek Him," is evident every morning when we open our eyes. I'm convinced when we see something that takes our breath, He smiles with pure love and says, *"I made that just for you."* When we look or listen to the birds, watch as the water cascades over the rocks in our various rivers, watch seasonally as the leaves constantly change colors or touch the very fabric of flower petals, we should remember this all comes from the creative hands of our Heavenly Father. I often bow my head in quiet adoration and gratitude, as I know we all do, to whisper, "Precious God, how great Thou art!."

And since Easter is the start of renewal, I was thinking this morning what we could all accomplish by letting go of the past and forgiving the ones who have hurt us. Stop thinking we're the only person from a broken home or a victim of spousal abuse, the only one with a void in our heart knowing we're going home to an empty house, and the list goes on. The world is full of pain and anxieties. We can change this, one person at a time, and that person starts with us. We can learn to love and smile from within, this is where it counts, deep down in our soul. Everyday we should expect the best from ourselves, our jobs and the people around us. Don't say, I think today is going to be better, say, I **know** today is going to be better.

Our prayer today: Dear Heavenly Father, thank You for dying for us, no greater love can man ever show. Please help us to remember, the happiest people on this earth are those who do the most for others. We ask and receive these things in the name of Jesus. Amen.

Khalid Ghamdi

Life's Challenges

With all the hatred and specially the killing of innocent children in the world today, I'm sure I'm not the only one asking "what's wrong with people." Some of us are too tense, anxious and concerned about things we have absolutely no control over. When we worry we become separated from God and before we know it we have lost all perception of right and wrong. As a young child did you ever notice the disappointment or hurt in your fathers' face when you did something wrong or out of character? Parents try so hard to teach us the right way, so, one can only imagine the yearning in our Fathers' face when He sees us struggling and searching for answers when all He has commanded us to do is come to Him. He tells us this in Matthew 11: 28-29 *"Come to Me, all you who labor and are heavy laden, and I will give you rest. Take My yoke upon you and learn from Me, for I am gentle and lowly in heart, and you will find rest for your souls."*

When our souls are at their lowest, let's get up, have a good laugh and find someone to do something nice too. Most of us never stop and think about how many people are out there who need our help. By putting others first in our lives, we are helping ourselves as well. The person who lives for others is the happiest. Happy people make better employees, better fathers, better mothers and better citizens. I heard a story, a true story, concerning a man in an airport whose flight had been cancelled, he had argued with the attendants at the ticket counter because they wouldn't reimburse him for what was going to be his overnight fare at a local hotel. He rode the escalator, still stewing, down to the ground floor where he noticed a lady with a small little girl just sitting there. As he made his way over to her he sensed something was wrong and in conversation, he realized the two hundred dollars a night for a hotel room in New York might as well had been two thousand. You see her child is very sick and they have to fly to New York, ever so often, where the little girl's specialist is. Her insurance doesn't pay for this so when ask if she would take a free round trip air fare for her seat being bumped, of course she agreed, never realizing that flight would be cancelled until the next day. Feeling ashamed of the way he handled his situation, he was humbled as a Christian and insisted on paying for her and her little girl's overnight stay, no strings attached, no exchanging of addresses. All she could get him to tell her was, he lived in Indiana and was an attorney. God has a way of bringing us back to reality and notice how all of this just seemed coincidental, things don't **just** happen when God's involved.

Our prayer today: God, may I always remember to love my neighbor, help the ones in need and be a refuge for the lonely. We all need each other to survive and for our well being. Lord, I pray for the sick and hurting, may Your touch and loving hands always be on them. Amen

Psalm 49: 1 & 2, 6 & 7, *"Hear this, all you people; Give ear, all you inhabitants of the world, low and high, rich and poor together."* *Those who trust in their wealth and boast in the multitude of their riches, none of them can by any means redeem his brother."*

Many of us have read the poem called Hector the Collector which pretty much sums up how God must feel about the things we think are precious.

Hector the Collector collected bits of string, collected dolls with broken heads and rusty bells that would not ring.

Pieces out of picture puzzles, bent-up nails and ice-cream sticks, twists of wires, worm-out tires, paper bags and broken bricks.

Old chipped vases, half shoelaces, Gatling guns that wouldn't shoot, leaky boats that wouldn't float and stopped-up horns what wouldn't toot.

Butter knives that had no handles, copper keys that fit no locks, rings that were to small for fingers, dried-up leaves and patched-up socks.

Worn-out belts that had no buckles, 'lectric trains that had no tracks, airplane models, broken bottles, three-legged chairs and cups with cracks.

Hector the Collector loved these things with all his soul, loved them more than shining diamonds, loved them more than glistening gold.

Hector called to all the people, "come and share my treasure trunk!" And all the silly sightless people came and looked...and called it junk.

Of all the "stuff" we have collected and stowed away as our legacy, what is it really worth to our Heavenly Father. He walks on the purest gold everyday, we hold on to ours with such joy, we insure it. In Matthew 16:26 *"What will a man give in exchange for his soul?"* Jesus said that the whole world fades in comparison to the value of a soul. We are worth more to our Creator than this world could ever give us. This reminds me of a large church in Atlanta paying a special tribute to one of their retired pastors, he was 92. After a warm welcome, introduction of this speaker, and as the applause quieted down, he rose from his high back chair and walked slowly, with great effort, to the podium.

"When I was asked to come here today and talk to you, your pastor asked me to tell you what was the greatest lesson ever learned in my 50 odd years of preaching. I thought about it for a few days and boiled it down to just one thing that made the most difference in my life and sustained me through all my trials. The one thing that I could always rely on when tears and heartbreak and pain and fear and sorrow paralyzed me...the only thing that would comfort was this verse...'Jesus loves me this I know. For the Bible tells me so."

When he finished, the church was quiet. You actually could hear his foot steps as he shuffled back to his chair. You see...he summed it all up for all of us...nothing compares or is as important as God's love for us and the Bible does tell us this, over and over. Lets please take just a little time from our busy schedules and reflect on the only thing we have no one can take away and all it costs is our love back.

Our prayer today: I do know You love me and I thank You with all my being. Thank You for giving Your Son as my ransom. Hold the sick and hurting close and breathe Your healing powers over them, ease their pain and suffering. Protect the children and elderly of this world and keep them safe. I ask this in the name of Jesus. Amen

Matthew 12: 34-37 *"For out of the abundance of the heart the mouth speaks. A good man out of the good treasure of his heart brings forth good things, and an evil man out of the evil treasure brings forth evil things. But I say to you for every idle word men may speak, they will give account of it in the day of judgment.. For by your words you will be justified, and by your words you will be condemned."*

How many times have you heard someone say, I wish I had. To me these are the saddest words in our vocabulary, the total helplessness and despair one feels when they're spoken. When tragedy hits and you see someone sitting all alone, the first words you will hear is..." I wish I had"... over and over. I can only imagine how many times they have been spoken during our recent tornados, the cyclone in Myanmar and the earthquake in China. Such devastation, our minds cannot comprehend. Most of us have never witnessed human loss on this scale and I sincerely hope we never do.

As I prayed for and cried with these survivors last evening I was reminded that our brains work a lot like a computer. What we put on the hard drive of our heart will show up on the monitor of our mouth. Sometimes we get so focused on ourselves and what's in it for me, that we forget our Godly inheritance to think of and help others. But the good thing is we can reprogram our thought process the same as we reprogram our computers. The Bible says our minds are renewed by the

Word of God. The more we read and study His Word, the more we will be transformed from the inside out. We can't always see our faults but we can ask our Heavenly Father to reveal to us the wrongs in our heart and to replace them with good treasures. Let the words we speak be a blessing to someone.

Many years ago my father and mother were taken to their new home in Heaven, this left their five children to fend for themselves. I used the word "fend" because it doesn't matter how old you get, you never lose the need for your parents. The comfort of being able to say, "I'll ask dad" or "call mom, she'll know." But out of this I learned to reprogram my computer, it taught me to never end a call, an email or letter without saying "I love you." If I talk to my boys, grandchildren or one of my siblings, I always tell them I love you. I may converse with them two or three times a day, I still end with, I love you. I never want to have to say, "I wish I had."

So today my wish for each of you is to please hold your children, spouse, mom or dad, just a little closer and don't just expect them to know how you feel, tell them. Use your monitor mouth to say, I love you so much. Whatever task is taking up your time will be there later, your loved one might not.

Our prayer today: Father in heaven, I humbly come before You and ask that You cleanse my heart and mind of anything that isn't pleasing to You. Fill me with Your faith and love that I might overflow with Your goodness today. I pray, hold each person going through today's worldwide tragedies so close they will be able to feel Your very presence. Blow Your healing breath over the sick and hurting and remind Your angels to keep the wall around the children and elderly of this world. I ask these thing in Jesus name. Amen

I was standing in line at one of our department stores, where they have thirty registers with only ten open, but this too was as God planned. There was a man and woman, I presume husband and wife, behind me so I could hear every word. It was evident they were in some kind of stress and didn't know what to do or where to turn. I wanted to turn around and ask what are you doing to yourselves, give this to the Lord and forget about it. He already knows our problems but He wants us to acknowledge Him and receive His grace. Not knowing these two, I smiled and whispered, it's going to be alright. They both smiled back and said "thank you." I guess they could see I had already asked God to intervene. In my thought process, and I'm sure yours also, I don't understand how anyone can start, go through or end a day without His amazing love. I have to know and feel He is near at all times so I can talk to Him. I've had people ask me, talking to yourself again? No, I smile and reply, just me and the Lord having a little conversation.

Proverbs 3: 5-6, *"Trust in the Lord with all your heart, and lean not on your own understanding; In all your ways acknowledge Him and He shall direct your paths. "* This brings to mind the saying, God gave me a mountain this time. Sometimes it does seem as though we will never enjoy the life the bible speaks of, but we can by adding the finishing words, "God gave me this mountain and by taking His hand He'll lead me to the top." He's our pick and safety rope; He won't let us fall. But there again, we must first do our part, He's not going to intrude or interfere. Sometimes I picture our Heavenly Father with His arms stretched out to a person using His name in vain and it breaks my heart, but then this is our God who loves us unconditionally. He patiently waits for us to invite Him in.

Prayer is the soil in which hope and healing grow best.

Our prayer today: God, I want to live for your approval alone. I need to feel Your presence and strength when I'm down and alone. I need to remember You love me just the way I am. Hold the sick and hurting close and make them feel Your love as You breathe over them. I pray this in the name of our loving Jesus. Amen and Amen.

John 16:33, *"These things I have spoken to you, that in Me you may have peace. In the world you will have tribulations; but be of good cheer, I have overcome the world. "*

In today's troubling times, I cannot, hard as I try, honestly believe there's anyone who doesn't, deep down in the pit of their soul, believe in our Heavenly Savior. Oh, we have protestors and prideful people who would like to think they're fooling the world, but just let one catastrophic thing happen in their lives and the first words out of their mouths is, "Oh, God help me." How sad their pitiful lives and what a waste to go through even one day not enjoying the goodness of our Lord . I am so happy when I open my eyes every morning, I look out the window and up at the sky. While I thank Him for His gift to me of another new day and the vision to see His greatness all around me, I survey the clouds looking for any glimpse of Him or one of His angels.

To many people are filled with fear, afraid of what might happen, when most of the time it never does. We make problems where none exist and in some cases make ourselves sick to the point of seeing a doctor or being hospitalized. This is the work of satan, and as His word says, you will have tribulations, but they are not to get us down, we need to lift our voices in thanks and praise. The Scriptures say that He has already overcome fear for us. Instead of choosing to live in fear, we need to choose to live in faith. The world may be full of hatred for every tribe of mankind, but God is bigger than all the troubles that are now and are yet to come in our lives. We should sleep sound at night knowing this, using His word as our pillow.

John 14: 1, 3, *"Let not your heart be troubled, you believe in God, believe also in Me...I will come again and receive you to myself; that where I am, there you may be also.* Such comforting words, "let not your heart be troubled." Could we please try to remember this the next time the world starts closing in around us? Lets practice saying it over and over until it's our first line of defense.

Our prayer today: Thank You Lord for giving me the comfort and security of Your love and the peace knowing Your Word is truth. Give me the boldness and strength not to live in fear. I do know you are bigger than any problem this world can or ever will hand me. Help me Lord to always be a light to others for Your goodness and glory to shine through. Hold the sick and hurting close and blow Your healing breath over them. This I ask in the name of Your son Jesus. Amen and Amen.

Have you ever listened to a person talk in defiant despair and you caught yourself smiling at them? I did this recently during a family get together because in my mind I could see what was about to happen to this person. One good thing I have learned is we can't run from ourselves, it doesn't matter where we go or what we do, guess what...there we are. So we might as well just settle back and be content with our company. I heard the words, "every time I think I'm about to reach the top, I slide back down, so where is this almighty God we're all suppose to believe in?" I thought, my dear sweet child, you're about to find out. The devil is slowly beating you down to your knees, right where God wants you, your life is about to take a delightful turn. There's some things mortal man or satan have no control over and our precious Redeemer loving us is one of them. When you reach the bottom and cry out, He's going to lift you up, wipe your slate clean and give you an inner peace only His touch can provide.

Psalm 121: 1-2 reads *I lift up my eyes to the hills-where does my help come from? My help comes from the LORD, the Maker of heaven and earth ."* And then in Philippians 3:13-14, *but this one thing I do, forgetting those things which are behind and reaching forward to what lies ahead, I press toward the mark for the prize of the high calling of God in Christ Jesus. "*

Yesterday is gone, we can't bring it back, tomorrow may not ever come, so why aren't we living like this is our last day on earth? We need to be walking just a little lighter on our feet, speaking to everyone we meet and taking in the smells of the air filled with fragrances from flowers, grass, trees, rain and yes even pollution. I started really appreciating all the senses God gave me when I heard a blind author talking about the 16 different grades of sand on the beach, can you imagine this, something we have all walked on, picked up, even built castles on and we didn't know. I remember thinking, this blind man knows more about God's creations than we do, things we take for granted, yet we know nothing about. Could it be we also take God for granted, this Savior who thought of us when He was designing the universe. All one has to do is simply stop, look around and take a deep breath to feel His love. So the next time we see someone hurting, we might want to suggest they reach for the hand of their Creator, give Him their problems and get on with what He wants us to do, enjoy the life He lovingly gave us.

Our prayer today: Heavenly Father, thank You for the gift of forgiveness, the gift that releases me from the past and enables me to run towards You and the bright future You have in store for me. God I know looking to You will solve all of life's issues. Thank You for giving me the answers and being there in my time of need. Amen.

This week some of us had to take a refresher course on Building Relationships at the workplace, which is a good thing because we're here with each other more than at home with our families. But it also brought to mind the relationship God desires to have with us. Remember that word desires, the dictionary says it means to long for. God longs for our attention and affection, He waits for us to invite Him in, this God who created the universe, we're talking about the moon, sun, stars, planets and the heavens. This God who gave us the trees to keep us cool, birds for music, flowers to perfume the air, clouds to amaze us as they form different figures and the oceans to calm the noise of the day. Just as we should write down the needs and characteristics of our fellow workers, we need to write down the good things God does for us daily.

Begin to focus on the victories and blessings in your life or as I like to say, the winks you receive from God everyday. When you see something that takes your breath away or you avoid a collision with another person, your child looks into your eyes and says, Mommy I love you or maybe your spouse decides the family should go out for dinner...that's a God wink. When you make an account of His goodness, you will quickly discover that He is working in you, *"to do exceeding abundantly above all that we ask or think."* Ephesians 3:20. Take a moment everyday to thank the Lord for all He's done for you. When we develop a thankful and caring heart, we are changing our focus from how big our problems are to how big our God is. Please, please, always remember, God loves us, all we have to do is think of the cross to know this.

Our prayer today: God, I praise you for life-changing powers and unconditional love. I want to give new life to my relationship with You so that others might see the love I have for You and that You live in my heart. Amen

Ephesians 2:22, *"In Him, and in fellowship with one another, you yourselves are also being built up. "* Psalm 133:1
*Behold, how good and how pleasant it is for brethren to dwell
together in unity. "* Colossians 3:8, 9, 10, *"But now you must
also put off all these: anger, wrath, malice, blasphemy, filthy
language out of your mouth. Do not lie to one another, since
you have put off the old man with his deeds, and put on the
new man who is renewed in knowledge according to the image
of Him who created him. "*

Imagine, when you and a group or simply another person dwell together in unity, it brings joy to the heart
of our Heavenly Father and strengthens us as well. In
today's world it is so important to find a church home
where we can participate in worship, fellowship, events,
small groups and outreach opportunities. We have to
clean our thought process of all the ugly, coming at us
from all directions.

Profanity and crude language is becoming more common on prime-time television programs. Many writers
and producers seem to intentionally push the limits of
immoral and offensive speech to see just how much the
public will allow. It's as though they're waiting for us to
stand up and say enough is enough. This is what our
children are hearing and seeing, from the time they get
up until they go to bed. This dishonors God and de-
grades both men and women. Conversations punctuated
by cursing, swear words, and last but not least, crude

and dirty expressions. Words that condemn others can inflame anger and destroy relationships. We should always try and remember, one can't erase what they hear.

Ungodly language creates an immoral and unspiritual atmosphere, which is hostile to clean thinking and living. If we allow ourselves to continually hear and live with this, we might find ourselves asking, how did I get here? Satan is always setting a trap for us, this is why we have to daily renew our minds with the Word of God. He gives the blueprint for the course of action we need to live clean and in Him.

In Psalm 141:3 we read and should practice everyday, *"Set a guard, O Lord, over my mouth; keep watch over the door to my lips."* This prayer is needed today more than ever. Profanity disgraces the user and demeans the hearer. Lets always set a good example of our walk with our Heavenly Father.

Our prayer today: God, I pray for the church today, without a place to dwell with other believers, I would grow weak. I pray for all my brothers and sisters that I fellowship with daily and some weekly. I do ask for You to help me guard my every word and be a blessing to others. I ask this in the name of Jesus. Amen

Deuteronomy 30:19, *"I call heaven and earth as witnesses today against you, that I have set before you life and death, blessing and cursing; therefore choose life, that both you and your descendant's may live."*
James 1: 13-15-16, *"Let no man say when he is tempted, I am tempted by God; for God cannot be tempted by evil, nor does He Himself tempt anyone. But each one is tempted when he is drawn away by his own desires and enticed. Then, when desire has conceived, it gives birth to sin; and sin, when it is full-grown, bring forth death. Do not be deceived, my beloved brethren."*

It seems as though more and more high profile people are being exposed for their wrong doings. This morning I saw a mug shot of our sweet Mary Ann of the hit show Gilligan's Island on the news for drug possession. Some of our past presidents, the governor of New York, government officials, several top singers and movie stars are being caught everyday , but not Mary Ann. Not only does these people hurt us, they're taking the very heart out of their families. It seems the devil is trying his best to destroy everything good in this world. Maybe we should read John 10:10 again. This tells us exactly what the devil is capable of doing, but it also reminds us of God's power and love.

Now is the time we must keep the right focus. God does not bring on, or put these situations into our lives. Can God keep these things from happening in our lives? Certainly

He can! But, if He did, He would go against His own law that He put into effect at the start of creation...that is, "freedom of choice." I feel once we step off into the wrong direction, He will use this trial in our lives to develop patience. Why do we need patience, we need forgiveness more wouldn't you say, while this is true, we need patience to wait on God to answer our prayers and to remember... He is God. He doesn't use the same calendar or clock as we do, maybe this is where much of the misconception comes from that God puts these things on us. He went through a brutal death on the cross for our sins and then to think He would deliberately punish us is beyond my comprehension. If we would show Him one ounce of the love He shows us, this world could be heaven on earth. The next time you're in an uncomfortable situation, please look around at all God has put here purely for your enjoyment and start praising Him and forget about your problem, He'll take care of it in His time.

Our prayer today: God, thank You for loving me more than I deserve, thank You for dying on the cross for my sins, thank You for claiming me as Yours. Dear Savior I pray, hold the families together, this world is so torn apart because of the lack of the family unit today. Children are left alone to fend for themselves the best they know how, which is seldom good. Have Your army of angels form a fence around each of them, protect and feed them with Your love. I humbly ask this in the name of Jesus...Amen and Amen

Romans 2: 15 & 16, *"who show the work of the law written in their hearts, their conscience also bearing witness, and between themselves their thoughts accusing or else excusing them. In the day when God will judge the secrets of men by Jesus Christ, according to my gospel."*

Galatians 6: 8, 9 10, *"For he who sows to his flesh will of the flesh reap corruption, but he who sows to the Spirit will of the Spirit reap everlasting life. And let us not grow weary while doing good, for in due season we shall reap if we do not lose heart. Therefore, as we have opportunity, let us do good to all, especially to those who are of the household of faith."*

So much of the time, we read about forgiveness and how it sets the prisoner free, the prisoner being us. I remember reading a story, while in high school, written by William Shakespeare in the 1600's named Macbeth and it came to me, how this is happening everyday in every part of our society . Lady Macbeth was greedy and power hungry. Having heard a prophecy that her husband would become king, she convinced him to as-sassinate the reigning monarch. When the bloody deed was done Macbeth was conscience-stricken. His wife re-sented his squeamishness and helped him cover up the crime. Her husband was crowned king, but that wasn't the end.

Lady Macbeth's initial resolve turned to remorse. She grew mentally unstable and couldn't stop washing her hands. "Will these hands ne'er be clean?" she asked. Finally, the guilt drove Lady Macbeth to suicide.

Guilt is an emotion that can weigh us down whenever we cross a moral boundary. All of us are capable of feeling guilty when we violate the law of God written in our hearts. If we continue to sin willfully, however, we will dull our conscience.

Lady Macbeth is a good reminder of biblical principle: Whatever we sow, we will certainly reap. When we feel temptation, we need to listen to our conscience-not try to silence it. It's far better to avoid committing an act we will later regret than live with the consequences.

Sometimes there's just one step to go before we yield to sin, but God will help us to say no if we trust His power within. This being Easter Sunday we should all remember, only the blood of Jesus can wash away the stains of sin.

Our prayer today: Thank You for forgiving me and giving me new life. I choose today to extend the gift of forgiveness to others. I bless those who have wronged me and ask You to heal every broken place in my life. Protect the helpless children and elderly of this world and keep them safe from all harm. Heal the sick and hurting, remove their pain, I pray. I ask these things in the name of Jesus. Amen.

Matthew 23: 9-12, *"Do not call anyone on earth your father; for One is your father, He who is in heaven. And do not be called teacher; for One is your Teacher; the Christ. But, who is greater among you shall be your servant. And whoever exalts himself will be abased, and he who humbles himself will be exalted."*

As I sat in my diversity training class yesterday, one common thread was apparent, all we want is to be recognized and appreciated for who we are. It doesn't matter if we're young or old, rich or poor, or what country we're from, just acknowledge I'm here. In Ephesians 2:22 we learn *"In Him, and in fellowship with one another, you yourselves are also being built up."* Our words have the power to pollute or purify. If we constantly complain we not only bring those around us down, but we ourselves take on an entirely different look, walk and attitude. What we forget sometimes is that complaining is based on the attitude of our heart, not our circumstances. When we stay focused on what's really important and have a heart full of gratitude, we don't have time to complain. It's only by His Grace we are even here; this should be enough to get us excited.

Matthew 13:8, *Other seed fell on good soil, where it produced a crop a hundred, sixty or thirty times what was sown."* This is the seed of God's Word, and as we sow good seeds into the fields of hurting and desperate people, they will find something to believe in and hold on to also. If we refer back to the scripture in the first paragraph, Jesus Himself promises we will reap a harvest that is beyond our expectations. When we go about doing His work, this brings joy to the heart of our Heavenly Father and strengthens us as well. There's plenty of soil for us to sow in, and a lot of it is right where we live and work. Our Almighty God is a giver and a servant; surely we don't think we are above Him. If the King of kings can wash His disciples' feet, then I think just maybe we can stop for one minute to offer kindness or a helping hand to our fellowman. Matthew 23:11 says *"He who is greatest among you shall be your servant."* I know we all want to be more like Him, now it's time to put our best intentions to practice. If God controls us on the inside, we'll be genuine on the outside.

Our prayer today: Dear God, I must confess I don't always have a positive attitude, I let negative thoughts, which is no more than the devil, poison me and those around me. I ask for forgiveness and help me to be a joy to those I meet on a daily bases and to be thankful in every situation. I always want to look for the good in everything and bring out the best in people. I ask this in the name of Your son Jesus. Amen.

Genesis 1:1-2, *In the beginning God created the heavens and the earth. The earth was without form and void; and darkness was on the face of the deep. And the spirit of God was hovering over the face of the waters.*
Isaiah 53: 5-6, *But He was wounded for our transgressions, He was bruised for our iniquities; The chastisement for our peace was upon Him, and by His stripes we are healed. All we like sheep have gone astray; We have turned, every one, to his own way; And the Lord has laid on Him the iniquity of us all.*

A man who was deeply troubled by his sins was having a vivid dream in which he saw Jesus being savagely whipped by a soldier. As the cruel scourge came down upon Christ's back, the onlooker shuddered, for the terrible cords left ugly, gaping wounds upon His bleeding and swollen body. When the soldier raised his arm to strike the Lord again, the man rushed forward to stop him. When he did, the wielder turned toward him and the dreamer was startled to see his own face!

How true is this today? Every time we commit a sin we just laid a stripe on Christ's back. As in Genesis, the earth was without form and void, so we didn't just happen, life has not always been here. God, the miracle maker, took nothing and turned it in to something. He took a grain of sand, made you and me with tender care and love, even before we were a twinkle in our dad's eye, God knew us and had already made plans for our lives.

But He also gave us the freedom of choice and choose we did. From the grain of sand to the shedding of His Son's blood, it was all for us. How wonderful that the Lord Jesus suffered and died to redeem a sinful and lost world! In one sense, Good Friday was the darkest day in human history. But because of Jesus' sacrifice for us, the cross was actually the greatest victory of all the ages. He didn't die just for someone else's sins, He died for you and me. The pain He endured says volumes about the extreme sinful nature of our own needs. Before you break one of His commandments, stop and think, would I hit Jesus with a whip and tear open His flesh? No, of course not, but isn't this actually what we're doing? Each time we deliberately do something wrong, we're walking up skull hill and spitting in the face of our Savior hanging there on the cross; we all know, nails didn't hold Him there, it was His unconditional love.

The next time you start to feel down and worthless, remember, someone died for you. The Creator of all the universe thought about you and gave you life, he decided the color of your hair, your eyes, even you skin, can't you just picture Him smiling as He made you, holding you in His massive hands as if you were a doll, how important is that? When you look around at the different colors of the clouds, trees, flowers, even the animals and birds, it's all for you. This should make all of us walk a little taller and have a smile even if we're alone.   We are so very special and the apple of our Father's eye.

Our prayer today: Father in Heaven, we never want to stop thanking You for the price You paid for us, even though we are so easily distracted. Please help us today to renew our gratitude for Your Son's death. Please use the surrender of this moment to let His life and Yours, be seen in us. Father we pray, protect the children and elderly from harm and abuse, feed them with Your love and kindness. We ask these things in the name of Jesus. Amen

Romans 12:3, "For by the grace given me I say to every one of you: Do not think of yourself more highly than you ought, but rather think of yourself with sober judgment, in accordance with the measure of faith God has given you."
Romans 13:1, "Everyone must submit himself to the governing authorities, for there is no authority except that which God has established. The authorities that exist have been established by God."

In today's world, for most of us, all we hear or read, woe unto me, with man it may be, but with God, ALL, things are possible. The first step we must take, is a step back. We have to remember who the highest God is and where we actually fit in His great plan. When we learn to take ourselves out of our lime light and off the pedestal we enjoy sitting on, or in other words, stop being a legend in "our" own minds, then we will humble ourselves and receive the inner comfort we so desperately need. I caught myself this past week in a down and out condition, "woe is me, what am I going to do." You know the routine, you worry a little, cry a river thinking, why me? Finally it dawns on you, why am I doing this to myself, all the while that slimy rabid dog Satan is having a field day at your expense. I don't think anything makes him any happier than to see our faces swollen from crying or the hurting in the pit of our stomachs from worrying about something we have no control over.

One moment in our helpless situation the light finally comes on, our God can handle anything, anytime, forget you devil, you're outa here. When we remove ourselves from the control panel and allow our Precious Father to take command, life is good. He has a plan to give us a way out, He will make things that seem impossible, possible. The Bible says that He has plans for our good, not for evil, to give us hope for our future. All we have to do is start believing and confessing, "I am with God and with Him all things are possible." When we stop and think about it, how simply is this, we have a loving Father who wants to handle all our fears and erase our problems. All we have to do is demote ourselves and put Him first. As we meditate on God's awesome power, He will work in our lives and we'll step forward into that place of victory He has in store for us.

I have come to a point in my walk with Him that now my little computer bank comes on when a problem arises and reminds me, tears cleanse the soul, worry separates me from God. I never intend to step off the path He has for me and He is always first in my thought process, He is the all knowing, all mighty God. He is Lord, which means Boss and I so enjoy being His servant and obeying His command.

Our prayer today: Heavenly Father, thank You for loving me and giving me the comfort I so need day to day. I choose to trust You and I will never doubt Your possibilities. Show me Your power. Work through me to encourage those around me to trust You with every aspect of their being. Hold the sick and hurting close and put a smile of "knowing" on their faces. I ask this in the name of Jesus. Amen and Amen.

1 John 4:4 *"You are of God, little children and have overcome them, because He who is in you is greater than he who is in the world. "* James 5:16, *"The prayer of the righteous is powerful and effective. "*

As most of us are aware through the news media, we have an epidemic of abuse among our teenagers. This didn't just happen, it was put in place several years ago when their parents were being abused. We have a generation of dads and moms who were raised believing this was the norm, use loud foul language toward your spouse or partner and if that didn't work, then use physical force. Our teenagers are acting out what they have learned either from their parents or heaven help us, the television and computer.

As parents or soon to be parents, we need to set a standard before our children and the world that is beyond reproach. What was started with no thought of the consequences, can be reverse. We must instill in our children, after all they are our future, their net worth. They are our gift from our Heavenly Father and we adore and appreciate them with all our being. Fathers set the standard by asking your daughters out for a date, show them how they are to be treated and most of all, respected. Mothers take your sons out, ask them to open your door, allow them to order your meal if you're dining out, show them how to treat a lady. Not only will this teach them how to conduct themselves, but you'll also make beautiful memories. I realize this might be a little much if they're going to McDonalds, but good manners can be used anywhere. Try this and see what happens. What we're really doing is teaching them respect for self and the rules our Lord set down for us.

I have spent many, many hours on my knees as I know you have also, it's what we do as parents and the scripture James 5:16 came to mind. I do believe God looks after His own and when we lift His gifts, He so lovingly gave us, up to Him, I feel in my heart He answers. It rips at the very core of my soul when I hear of a child being abused or witness how some young people treat each other. This reminds me of how far we still have to go. If we could just start today practicing showing the love our Father has shown us, I think we could see a big change in our society.

Our prayer today: Dear Heavenly Father, thank You for giving me the gift of my children. Help me to instill in them the values You set at the beginning of time. You made all of us in Your image and I pray that I can focus on all that is honorable and good and my children will learn from my actions. Hold the sick and hurting close and breathe Your healing powers over them. I ask this in the name of Jesus. Amen.

John 10:4, *"And when he brings out his own sheep, he goes before them; and the sheep follow him, for they know his voice."*

I found this story that I wanted to share with you today, because, it reminds us to always listen for our Savior's voice. After a hijacked plane slammed into the Pentagon on September 11, 2001, many people inside the building we trapped by a cloud of thick blinding smoke. Police officer Isaac Hoopi ran into the blackness, searching for survivors, and heard people calling for help. He began shouting back, over and over, "Head toward my voice! Head toward my voice!"

Six people, who had lost all sense of direction in a smoke-filled hallway, heard the officer's shouts and followed. Hoopi's voice led them out of the building to safety.

"Head toward My voice!" That's also the invitation of Jesus to each of us when we are in danger or when we have lost our way. Jesus described the true spiritual shepherd of the sheep as one who "calls his own sheep by name and leads them out." Are we listening for Jesus' voice during our times of prayer and mediation? When we're in difficult circumstances, are we walking toward Him, reaching for His hand and guidance or do we just keep going around the same mountain making the ruts deeper and deeper? You know I heard a song that says "I saw God today." We see God everyday, even

in the night, all we have to do is look. The clouds were
so pretty yesterday as I came in to work, I remarked
to a co-worker who was also looking at the sky, "have
you ever seen a masterpiece such as this with only two
colors?" The brush strokes were very definite and the
color of soft pink against the light blue sky was breath
taking. There He was for all to see saying, "this is how
much I love you."

When you hear the Shepherd's voice as He calls you,
"Come to Me," in your life make Him your choice and
a faithful follower be. What this conveys is, you don't
need to know where you're going if you're following the
Shepherd. Let's keep Him first in our thought 24/7;
after all, that's where He belongs.

Our prayer today: Precious Father thank You for filling
my eyes each day with new sights and my heart with new
joys, Your beauty is everywhere. Help me to always put
You first in everything I do and to be a witness for Your
goodness. Hold the sick and hurting close and breathe
your healing powers over each of them, ease their pain
and suffering. We ask these things in the name of Jesus.
Amen

As with any growing company, people have to be relocated for expansion and to make room for future employees as with my employ recently. While cleaning out file cabinets I came across a story I had printed in '02, and after re-reading it, I now know why I thought this was something to save. I've learned as we grow in our walk with the Lord, He will show us the meanings for things that in the past would go right over our heads.

An Indian evangelist Sundar Singh wrote about a devastating forest fire in the Himalayas where he was traveling. While many were trying to fight it, a group of men stood looking up at a tree with flames climbing up its branches. They were watching a mother bird flying frantically in circles above the tree. She was chirping out an alarm to her nest full of fledglings. As the nest began to burn, the mother bird didn't fly away; instead she zoomed down and covered her brood with her wings. In seconds she and her nestlings were burned to ashes.

Singh then said to the awe-stricken spectators: "We have witnessed a truly marvelous thing. God created that bird with such love and devotion that she gave her life trying to protect her young. That is the love that brought Him down from heaven to become man. That is the love that made Him suffer a painful death for our sake. Which brings us to our scriptures for today, Psalm 91:4, *"He shall cover you with His feathers and under His wings you shall take refuge. "* Then in 1 Peter 2:24, *"who Himself bore our sins in His own body on the tree, that we, having died to sins, might live for righteousness...by whose stripes you were healed.* " Like the bird who could have flown away and saved herself, Christ could have left us to fend for ourselves. He knew what pain He would have to endure. In Matthew 26:39, *"He fell on His face and prayed saying, "O My Father, if it is possible, let this cup pass from Me; nevertheless, not as I will, but as You will."* Can we remember this the next time we complain about a little mountain in front of us, "not my will, but Yours O Lord."

Our prayer today: Lord, thank You for dying in our place. How grateful we are for all that You have done and continually do for us. Help us to never complain about the little bumps we encounter on this journey we call life. This is a mere dream, and one day, we will wake up sitting at Your feet. Hold the sick and hurting close and breathe Your healing love over them. Precious God we pray these things in the name of your Son Jesus... Amen and Amen.

I know most of us have had nights when we didn't get any sleep and it could be for any number of reasons, a sick child, parent or spouse, something we ate or maybe we heard something our computer memory can't let go of. Whatever the reason, we feel less than human all the next day, and we really want to have a pity party for one, but this is not to be, the world doesn't know, nor does it care, that we're functioning with toothpicks holding our eyes open. The more we think we're not going to make it through the day, the more determine we must become and put our trust and faith in God.

Psalm 118:24, *"This is the day which the Lord has made; Let us rejoice and be glad in it."* Notice the Bible didn't say, I might be glad today "if" everything goes like I want it to. Like a person best not get in my way while I'm working through this maze of traffic on my way to a job that I really don't like, where they don't appreciate or pay me enough or I wish I could afford a cleaning service for my dirty house or if only I could find the extra money I need to make myself look better. No, the Psalmist said, "I **will** rejoice and be glad." God, I thank You for this car I'm driving, I could be walking; thank You for the roof over my head, I could be homeless; thank You for the money to pay my bills which comes from my job where I'm going to try harder; and thank You for making me look just like you want me too, I am Your creation. No matter what kind of difficulties I face today, no matter who tries to get me upset, I choose to be happy. Never forget that although we might not be able to choose our circumstances, we can choose how we respond to them.

If we will make up our minds each morning to be happy and full of joy, the enemy can't keep us down and defeated. God will give us the strength we need to overcome any obstacle we face. We can live that life of victory He has in store for us. This life is our training ground for our future. We need to give it our best. We only get to go around one time.

Our prayer today: Thank You God for blessing me, my family and friends. Thank You for I know, without a doubt, I will retire with You in heaven. Hold the sick and hurting close and breathe Your healing power over them. We ask these things and give You thanks in the name of Your son Jesus. Amen

I don't know about you, but some nights I simply can't shut down my mind, it keeps racing with the events of the day, what lies ahead or what might happen, crazy isn't it? You close your eyes tight, thinking okay this will help me relax and go to sleep, after a few seconds you open one eye and say to yourself, just testing, am I getting sleepy?....not even close. This is when I say okay Lord, I'm going to need a few minutes of Your time, I want You to know just how thankful I am for all the things You allowed me to go through today, this was Your way of honing me. For all the beautiful things You put here for my eyes to see and for keeping me safe. This was Your way of letting me know how much You love me. When I pray this prayer it seems as though my computer brain starts to shutdown and a peace covers by body like a warm blanket.

So it's time to install the truth of God's Word onto the hard drive of our minds. As in Romans 12:2, *"Be transformed by the renewing of your mind."* I know this will help us, as night slowly envelops the light by saying, "thank You God for this day."

Proverbs 23:7 *"As a person thinks in his heart, so is he."* If we think about being like our Father and doing His work, then a lot of our problems would go away or never come to be. We tend to try and make others like we want them to be, but if we study His word, He wants us to be like Him, not like someone else. As Christ followers we are to "imitate Him" as stated in 1 Corinthians 11: 1, *"Imitate me, just as I also imitate Christ."* Does this mean we will all act the same? Yes and no. Yes in that our behavior toward each other will increasingly become more like those of Jesus. No, because we are all given different gifts, interests and abilities to develop for His glory. I guess we could understand it this way, what we think about ourselves, God, the world and our spirituality really makes us who we are. Jesus simply says, *"When you're ready to think like God thinks about all of life, download my Word...I am the way and the truth."* If only we would learn to treat and love each other the way He wants us to, we would have a better peace of mind and different attitudes. What a wonderful world this would be if there was no hatred, stealing or killing, where children could play with no fear, families really knew each other. When was the last time we actually took just five minutes to listen to our loved ones, young or old? God listens and don't we want to be more like Him? Of course, we all do.

Our prayer today: Dear God help us to always put Your thought process first, when we open our mouths let our hearts be pure. May we love others as You love us and I thank You for loving us. We are not worthy of touching the sandals on Your feet, yet You willingly died for us. Ease the pain of the sick and hurting we pray and we ask this in the name of Jesus...Amen

1 Samuel 16:7, *"The Lord does not look at the things man looks at. Man looks at the outward appearance, but the Lord looks at the heart."*

1 Thessalonians 2:13, *"We thank God continually because, when you received the Word of God, which you heard from us, you accepted it not as the word of man, but as it actually is, the Word of God which is at work in you who believe."*

When the Lord looks at your heart, what does He see? Every one has an outer life and an inner life. The outer life is our public life that everyone can see. Our inner life is made up of our thoughts, our attitudes and our motives.

I was waiting in line to grab a cup of go juice, Monday morning in our break room when one of the regulars boldly said, "how about putting a little hurry in it up there sis." We all just laughed, but then he started telling me I reminded him of an elderly lady he was behind in the grocery line. Now what do you think my first impulse was....you're right, however, I didn't. But then he began to tell me about the situation. The cashier gave the lady her total and then waited for the money. Being from the old school she wouldn't or didn't use a debit card, and after finally retrieving her checkbook from her oversized handbag, she then dropped her pen. Realizing no one was offering to help her, he jumped in front of the others. He picked it up and at that time, saw the disappointment on her face knowing she was holding everyone back. He said as my heart turned to mush, I smiled, handed her the pen and said "this one is on me sis."

Everyone in the room was totally silent when I told him how nice that was. He came back with, "wasn't nothing, I think it was like about $11.00." What "wasn't anything" to him will be remembered in the minds of many. We can only imagine how many people noticed his actions in the grocery line and told others. This brings to mind, only you and God know what's going on inside, but sometimes I've noticed God has to know what's going on, because I don't have a clue. Aren't we thankful we have finally learned to turn everything over to Him. When we are faithful to receive His Word, it opens the door for Him to work through us. Have you ever asked yourself, how did that happen? I have and then started looking back at the progression of steps, it was Him.

Our prayer today: Father in Heaven, thank You for working in my life. Thank You for loving me and setting me free. I ask today, search the deep places of my heart, show me if there is any area where I need to line up my heart with my actions. Help me to be authentic in You. I ask these things in the name of Jesus. Amen

Proverbs 16: 7-8, *"When a man's ways please the Lord, He makes even his enemies to be at peace with him. Better is a little with righteousness, than vast revenues without justice. "*

How many times have your dreams been diminished or totally erased by something someone said, whether with forethought or simply off the cuff, something that was forever stored in your computer memory? I think we say things to people trying to help them, or to protect them if you will, but rarely do we think about our words. God's word says our heart dictates what comes out of our mouths, but the ears of others might not have the same filtering system. What we mean with the purest intentions could be hurtful to someone else. Case in point, when I was displaced with First Union, I knew I had to find another job, and quickly, because for a few years I had been reminded of my age, which in today's world is a real issue, and I didn't want to become stale in the workplace. Long story short, I was out of work thirty days when I found another job within First Union which was a progression of God winks.

First of all I was the only one whose computer was left on when we were told of our dismissal. Second when I pulled up the job list there were three, however, my transmittal would only go through on one. Third, I received a call from a person I saw when I came for my interview and was told there were twenty other people ahead of me for the same position and not to get my

hopes up, remember your age. Well I took all of this
into consideration, got on my knees and said "Lord put
me where I can be of service to You." I feel in my heart,
that person didn't mean me any harm and if I didn't
trust the Lord with all of my being I might would have
given up, but the rest is history. We should never doubt
our Savior nor should we try to promote ourselves. All
we need to do is trust and let Him take the lead. Let's
also remember to be careful with our words, to always
build, not destroy. One word of praise can carry one a
long way but a hurtful word can stop one dead in their
tracks.

Our prayer today: Thank You Lord for placing me
where You want me to be. I want to fight the good fight
for righteousness and I want You to use me everyday for
Thy glory. Help me to stay the course by doing Your
will and staying in the Word. Hold the sick and hurting
close and ease their suffering and pain, shield the little
children and elderly with Your army of angels. We pray
this in the name of Your son, Jesus. Amen

I don't know where the first six months of this year have gone, I just know somewhere along the way I lost a few weeks. Don't you feel this way, we look around, we're in the last week of June, what happened to May? Did we skip it this year or were we all too busy to live each day as our God intended? So we take our vacations to unwind, just kick back, grab a good book, throw away our clocks, hide the TV remote, sit in a folding chair and watch the sunset, all the while holding on tight to our excess baggage. By this I mean the kind that weighs your heart down and that, if carried around, leaves you emotionally and spiritually exhausted. We didn't get the job promotion we knew we deserved, a trusted friend betrayed or unjustly caused us much pain, doesn't seem as though we will ever have all we know we're entitled too and the list goes on. All of these seem very natural to a fallen heart, but this can also lead us to making wrong choices. You see we all have this computer chip called self-protection so when we think too much we can sometimes come up with the choice "I don't get mad, I just get even", we know this is wrong.

In Isaiah 40:29, *"He gives strength to the weary and increases the power of the weak."* He also tells us to listen for his direction so sometimes when I realize I can't handle this by myself nor do I want to bother with it anymore, I'm sick to death of the whole thing I simply pray, "God, I need You to talk to me. I desperately need Your wisdom. You brought this into my life for a purpose, but I don't know what to do next." His instructions to us is the way He lived, "turn the other cheek," "go the extra mile," and to "bless those who curse you." Does this make us feel like a pushover or maybe being perceived as a weakling, could be , but God in His grace also reminds us of the surrender of Christ on the cross. For Jesus the path to glory was the path of surrender and letting go. God drew me to the point of decision once again. Am I going to try and manage this situation to my advantage or am I going to release it, in trust and obedience, to Him? Why don't we leave our excess baggage in the cabin atop a mountain, at Disney World or the sands of our beautiful beaches and let our Lord lighten our load. Surrender it to Him and let's do what He wants us to do, enjoy each and everyday, after all, it's His gift to us. It makes Him happy to see us happy, just like with our children or family. The greatest joy I have is giving to my family and friends, seeing the delight and smiles this brings.

Our prayer today: God thank you for answering prayers, for taking our problems and burdens so that we might live life to the fullest. Give us the wisdom and discernment to hear Your still, soft voice through the noise of this world. Hold the sick and hurting so close the pain and illness leaves their bodies. We pray this in the name of Jesus. Amen and Amen.

Today, I would like for us to take a moment, get a shovel and start digging out the one sin we have buried deeper and deeper trying to make it go away. The one that haunts us night and day and eats at the very core of our lives. We wake up with it; it follows us to work; it's with us at the dinner table and finally it goes to bed with us. We lie there asking God to please make this feeling go away for we know one day someone will find out and we're doomed, who would ever think we could stoop so low as to commit this sin. This brings us to fully understand Psalm 51:1-3, *Have mercy upon me, O God, according to Your loving kindness; According to the multitude of Your tender mercies, blot our my transgressions. Wash me thoroughly from my iniquity, and cleanse me from my sin. For I acknowledge my transgressions and my sin is ever before me.* "

I sat and listened to a young man tell me about his deepest heartfelt problem. He said it came to the forefront while he was watching his son play tag football when all of a sudden he could see another little boy's figure running right along beside him. I wiped my eyes, he said, thinking they had become blurred and looked again, straining to get a clearer picture. "Oh, dear God, I thought....it's him." This young man was sobbing uncontrollably still trying to tell me about a mistake he and his girlfriend had made some years earlier. I forced her to have an abortion and if God would allow me to live it over again, He wouldn't have to be ashamed of me as I am of myself. I would love to meet her again and tell her just how sorry I am and to please, please forgive me. I put my arms around him and recited the words to one of my favorite songs: What can wash away my sins? Nothing but the blood of Jesus. What can make me whole again? Nothing but the blood of Jesus. God knows what we have done, He knows what we're going to do, and through all of this He still loves us and forgives us. what a Savior. The one thing we must learn is to let go of it ourselves. When we confess with our mouths and hearts, God wipes the slate clean and it is forgotten, never to be written against us again.

I told this young man, God is giving you the chance to be the best dad your son could ever hope for. Raise him in a Godly home with Godly parents so that he will do the same by his children. When we keep digging up our past, after we have asked God to forgive us, this is called separation from Christ, and we're our own worst enemy. I found this little poem and it certainly fits today: "He knows our burdens and our crosses. Those things that hurt, our trials and losses. He cares for every soul that cries. God wipes the tears from weeping eyes."

Our prayer today: Dear God, thank You for loving me more than my mind will ever comprehend, forgiving

me of my sins and never reminding me of them again.
I thank you for the beautiful clouds in the sky, I looked
at one this morning with a perfect square opening and
I thought, good morning Lord, I know You're watching
over me. I praise You in the name of Jesus...Amen

Try to think of the one thing in your daily life that is just plain hard to do...wait, right? We've all heard the prayer: "Dear God, make me more patient....and do it now!" Of all the spiritual virtues, patience is the one that gives me the most trouble. I feel as though my life is passing me by when I have to sit at a red light and watch it change three to five times before I get to go. Not only am I wasting gas but also precious time. Believe it or not, we all have the same amount of time in a day, it's how we spend it that makes the difference. The older we get the more we realize why time is so precious. How about the ones that change lanes at the supermarket, just to get to the express checkout with more than ten or 20 items, I might add, and they laugh and chit chat with the cashier so she won't notice she's already filled five bags and still has a half a cart to go. Since, I'm already telling you what raises my blood pressure, what really breaks me down is when I'm the one in the express lane with a cart load and someone comes up behind me with one or two items, I feel like a low dog. I sincerely smile and ask, "is that all you have, please get in front of me," of which I mean from my heart, then they'll say, are you sure? "Oh yes...please", I say in almost a pleading tone, you see, I want them to get in front before God speaks to me and I have to start looking for another cashier.

"They who wait for the Lord shall renew their strength." Isaiah 40:31. Patience is more than a virtue, it's a fruit of the Spirit. It reflects His very presence in our lives, for He is a patient God. If He weren't, we all would have been annihilated long ago. When life or people don't measure up to our expectations, being patient can be quite a challenge, but it's clear God wants us to develop this trait. I've often wondered why our struggle with patience can be unsuccessful sometimes, maybe it's because we focus on our own agendas and timelines and we stop trusting Him for our guidance. We might run into these holding patterns so He can simply teach us to be more concerned with the struggles and feelings of others rather than being totally absorbed in our own interests and plans. Or, it just may be that God wants to give us the opportunity to show what His patience is like by demonstrating it to others.

One thing we can rest assured in, God's time is always the right time. Whether we're in traffic or standing in the express line, His management of our situation is always the best management. Patience is not learning to wait for others, it's learning to wait on God and to cooperate with His work in our lives. So the next time you have to wait, wait to see what the Lord is saying to you. In serving the Lord, it's always too soon to quit.

I found this little poem I thought you might enjoy: "Whatever you're doing for Jesus today, Be sure to keep at it... don't stop or delay;' If you are discouraged, don't give up your place, For God will sustain you by His matchless grace. " I think this deserves an Amen and Amen.

I was reading in Romans when I came across this scripture in chapter 12:16 *"Live in harmony with one another."* How good does this sound? And then in Psalm 32:8, *"I will instruct you and teach you."* God's love is powerful, He is the presence of harmony and understanding that blesses all relationships. When we open our eyes, our first words should be, "good morning Lord, thank You for my gift of today", not, "oh good grief, it's only Wednesday." By centering our thoughts and feelings on His presence within us, we can get in touch with what's true and genuine, like listening to the news media tell us about the thousands of people throughout the world that didn't receive His gift of today. Now get to your feet, stumble to your bathroom, look straight in the mirror (please, give yourself a break, don't scream) and say God loves me...you didn't say it loud enough...point to the mirror, smile and say "GOD LOVES ME." Now doesn't that feel good and all the while you're thinking, "I don't know why He loves me, but I know He does." Not only is God's love powerful, it's also wonderful. When we accept His love we have a happier attitude and this makes us more approachable, people feel comfortable and secure around us, I guess you could say, we're letting our light shine.

Now this brings us to Matthew 18:21-22, *"Then Peter came to Him and said, "Lord how often shall my brother sin against me, and I forgive him? Up to seven times? Jesus said to him, "I do not say to you, up to seven times, but up to seventy times seven.*" Forgiveness is a daily practice of choosing to avoid harsh judgment and resentment, we are to show love and acceptance. I know for me when I forgive someone for hurtful untruths, I release unwanted hostilities and anguish that would only be a burden and spoil my entire day, which is totally unacceptable for as I said earlier, this day is special, it's a gift from our God. If we would only stop and think how insignificant these things are in the grand scheme of life, then we would see them for what they really are, just a minor inconvenience and not worthy of a second thought. After all when we refuse to forgive it only hurts us, so the next time someone either intentionally or unintentionally says or does something to hurt you, say "God I forgive them, as You have forgiven me." With a little practice and time we will learn to love ourselves and other people as God loves us. What more could we ask for, as a matter of testing ourselves, lets say it one more time...GOD LOVES ME. Just close your eyes, feel the warmth and comfort of His love as it covers your entire being.

"The greatness of our God is seen in sky and sea and forest green; And living creatures great and small, reveal the God who made them all." I remembered this today as I watched five young deer running across an open field just as I was leaving for work and I thought, thank you God for allowing me to see Your splendor this fine day.

Our prayer today: Thank you dear God for all Your wonderment and allowing us to be a part of Your universe...may we always remember to share the love You show us with our fellowman. We offer up praise to Your name. Amen.

Today, maybe we can start thinking about some of the words we use. Words are instruments we can use to build or destroy. The Bible encourages us to use our words to bless people. To bless means to speak well of, to pronounce favor, and to declare good things. All of us has someone who needs to receive our blessing, especially our families.

James 3:10 reads, *"Out of the same mouth we bless people, and we curse people, that should not be so."* Are we using the right words to build and not tear down, are we speaking love, affection and encouragement? I've heard people say, "well I wasn't shown love as a child and I turned out okay, who needs it anyway? If you listen to this person you will quickly see that thick wall he has built so no more hurt and loneliness can penetrate and most of the time these people don't realize how self protective they really are. Our words should come from our heart straight to the person needing it. You never know the power your words might have until you direct them with love and kindness. Lets decide today we are going to stop talking down to one another. We're going to choose instead to encourage each other. Stop focusing on what others are doing wrong and start thanking them for what they are doing right.

In Luke 6:38, we read when we give, no matter if it's words, smiles, money or kindness, it will be returned to us pressed down, shaken together and running over.

Our decision to have a positive influence will have a greater impact than we could ever imagine. As I was driving in this morning I was Praising God for my blessings, I was thinking, Lord my cup runneth over, thank You. This is God's word that He will give us blessings and joy unspeakable. Please always remember we can't out give God, the more we try, the more He gives back.

Our prayer today: God, I want to use words to bless, encourage and lift others up. Help me start my day with kindness in my heart. Give me uplifting words to say and the discipline to keep negative criticisms to myself. I pray this in the name of Jesus...Amen and Amen

1 Samuel 30: 6, *Then David was greatly distressed, for the people spoke of stoning him, because the soul of all the people was grieved, every man for his sons and his daughters. But David strengthened himself in the Lord his God.*
Joshua 1:9, *"Have I not commanded you? Be strong and of good courage; do not be afraid, nor be dismayed, for the Lord your God is with you wherever you go."*

As we read 1 Samuel, chapter 30 starting with verse 1, we understand why everything looked bleak to David and his men when they arrived at Ziklag. The Amalekites had attacked the city and taken their wives and children captive. The men were so discouraged they wept until they had no more energy. And David, being their leader, was greatly distressed, because the people were contemplating stoning him.

If you're anything like me, and I dare say we're all alike in more ways than we care to explain, I have cried until there were no more tears in me. The tear ducts were empty, but I've also learned, tears cleanse the soul. When the weeping is over, we think clearer, we know what we have to do. This is what happened to David and his army. They defeated the Amalekites and took back their families. David strengthened himself in the Lord his God. I've also seen the word strengthened translated to refreshed or encouraged. I have read this text many times and it doesn't exactly tell us how David did this. But it makes me wonder, in what ways can we strengthen, encourage, or refresh ourselves in the Lord when we're feeling discouraged.

Starting off this new year, the vast majority of us will face many mountains in these volatile times, but there's two things we can remember, this way we can keep things in perspective. First, we can remember what God has done already, how He has provided for us, how He answered or didn't answer our prayer requests. Some times we don't get what we ask for because it's not in our best interest. Second, we can remember what He promised in Joshua (9), *"Be strong and of good courage... for the Lord your God is with you wherever you go."* I like that word *"wherever"*, that means He's with us all the time.

Like David, let's learn to strengthen ourselves in the Lord, and then leave the rest to Him. I've learned when I lay problems at His feet, it's not wise to go back and try to pick them up again. So many times we tell our Father God, I can't handle this, you take it from me and then we try and help Him. When we face mountains, we can tell them to move, and if they don't, then we can just go over the top, He's always there.

Our prayer today: Father God, every morning when I open my gift of the day from you, I eagerly look forward to what You have in store for me. I thank You for planning my every move and keeping me on the path You have laid out for me. I ask these things in the name of Jesus. Amen.

Galatians 5:5, *"But by faith we eagerly await through the Spirit the righteousness for which we hope."* and then in Hebrews 11:1, *"Now faith is being sure of what we hope for and certain of what we do not see."*

Faith and hope is the same as goal and plan; we can't have one without the other. Faith and hope is something we can't see, but our every waking minute is, or should be, filled with it. A plan we can put on paper and then make a list of the goals we will need to achieve to make it happen, but if we aren't certain we can accomplish it, then we left out the most crucial part..... faith. The Bible says in Hebrews, "Now faith is..." in other words faith is always in the present. We get up every morning, without thinking, having faith our legs and feet will hold us up, the lights will come on when we flip the switch, water will come through the faucets, we'll see our families again at days end and God is going to take care of everything. Most of us never think about this being "faith", we just take it for granted, it is supposed to be. Why is it suppose to be.....simply because He loves us. Please right now, take a deep breath and say..."He loves me." Isn't this an awesome feeling?

In Matthew 9:29, *"According to your faith be it done unto you."* We can translate this to, "Have what your faith expects." We need to stop playing it safe, being afraid of uncertainties, failure and rejection. We can do this through faith...faith in our Almighty Savior. Has He ever let you down or did "you" turn away? You see hard as we try, we never let Him down, He knows what we're going to do or think before we ever do it, we're no surprise to Him. So many times I have caught myself trying to go it alone, not intentionally please understand, but all of a sudden realizing something's not quite right. Then it dawns on me, where do I have God in this equation? I laugh at myself thinking how foolish, or for a better view of the situation, what a nitwit I am, then I bow and humbly ask Him to take the reins.

Lets start expecting to overcome every challenge we face, start expecting God to meet our every need. We need to live filled with faith and anticipation that God is going to bless us beyond our wildest dreams and all we have to do is believe. What a great God we serve.

Our prayer today: Dear God, I want to grow even deeper in my faith. I believe You want the best for me. Help me to learn to expect to be blessed everyday and to face challenges with the confidence that You will see me through. You have always been there and Your Word says You always will be. I pray these things in the name of Your son, Jesus. Amen

I wanted to share with you a chance encounter I had with a person whom I consider a warm yet lonely individual. This has been in the making for two years now and the outcome shows how merciful our God really is. At the time this person had low, or I should say no, self esteem and my heart would break every time I saw her, until one day I couldn't stand it anymore, I asked her, when was the last time you felt love, the warm feeling knowing you're special? She looked at me and said, "all I've ever heard is, who would want you?" I quoted her Jeremiah 1:5, *Before you were ever formed in your mother's womb, I saw you and approved you.*" Do you know you are the apple of our Almighty God's eye, He made you in His image and loves you just the way you are, you're His most precious creation, now how awesome is that? There's enough power in these words for you, or any of us, to conquer the world. We should never let the enemy bring us down by trying to make us think we're not good enough, stand firm knowing we are approved and loved by the One that will never let us down. When people and negative thoughts start tearing at your soul, start praising the Lord, this works every time.

1 Corinthians 2:9 states, *"No man has ever seen, heard or even imagined the wonderful things God has in store for those who love the Lord."* No matter how bad you think things are for you right now, God has good in store for you. He'll take you to new levels, give you more wisdom and greater blessings than your human mind can

fathom. When we accept God as our personal Savior, our thoughts are purer, our vision becomes clearer and our actions imitates His. If you're waiting for me to say, and the end of this story is, it's not going to happen, you see this is just the beginning of the rest of her life. In the past she wasn't living but merely existing, now she has something to look forward too each day with great expectations. If we believe in our hearts that we can overcome, act like we can overcome, then we will overcome. We can be anything we want to be through the love of Jesus. Her smile is now one of joy, her eyes look directly at you and she is now working for her Lord. How great is that?

Our prayer today: Thank you Father for loving me with all my faults, You never put me down, You're always there to lift me up, take my hand Precious Lord and I will follow. Hold the sick and hurting close to Your bosom and ease their pain, give their families peace and strength. We pray these things in the name of Jesus... Amen

How many times have you opened your eyes and thanked God for His blessing of a new day. You're feeling good, even smiling at the dog, and then all of a sudden you notice you dropped your toothbrush on the floor and the five second rule doesn't apply here. You pick it up, run hot scalding water over it then rinse it with mouthwash. Now we'll finish brushing our teeth, take another sip of coffee, spit it out, MAN, that's hot. Still we're thinking, it's okay just routine stuff. Step in the shower, the liquid soap bottle slips through your fingers and it doesn't feel too good on top of your foot, now you start to think to yourself, "devil, you might as well go on somewhere else, you are not welcome here and I will not allow you to rob me of my joy."

Matthew 12:29 says, *"Or else how can one enter a strong man's house and plunder his goods, unless he first binds the strong man? And then he will plunder his house."* We have to set our minds to keep the devil from entering by speaking the words of God all the time. I don't know about you but we have now moved all our medicines to a cabinet in our kitchen, the medicine chest doesn't hold them anymore. It seems the older you get the more aches and pains you have to contend with and that's okay, it means we are still able to get around. A lot of people would love to trade places with us. So now you're in the kitchen to get your vitamins and other necessary pills to start your day, and what happens? You knock three or four bottles from the cabinet to the counter and then on to the floor where one of those child proof caps comes off. You're on your knees picking each expensive pill up saying, "devil, you're treading on thin ice." Then you're pouring your left over coffee in your thermos while at the same time emptying the grounds so the pot won't stain. Your arm ever so lightly touches the thermos and half of your wonderful coffee, sweetened with International Flavored creamer, is now on your stove. At this point I just started singing, "what can wash away my sins nothing but the blood of Jesus." I know in my heart, this day is going to be the best one yet, I am in God's favor.

Our prayer today: Dear Father, I thank You for the angel that hovers over me wherever I go or wherever I am. I do know she's there because I can definitely feel her presence and can almost see her. Thank You for this secure feeling and for loving me. Help me Lord to always curb my temper and my words, to always know You are near. Amen

Romans 8:28 *And we know that all things work together for the good to those who love God, to those who are the called according to His purpose.*

As we all know, everything works together for our good, maybe at the time we're so absorbed in the moment, we can't possibly imagine that it could, but when it's all over and we look back, it's perfectly clear.

Over 100 years ago, a tornado struck the prairies of Minnesota. Many were killed, hundreds were injured and one small town was almost blown away. In the midst of the disaster, an elderly British surgeon and his two medically trained sons worked around the clock for days taking care of the sick, bandaging wounds, and setting broken limbs.

This wonderful act of kindness did not go unnoticed. The doctor and his sons were offered financial backing to build a hospital. The men agreed and in 1889 founded a clinic. You might know the rest of the story, the elderly doctor's name: William W. Mayo.

From a great tragedy the Mayo Clinic was born. It now consists of over 500 physicians treating more than 200,000 people a year and is known worldwide as one of the premiere clinics of health and excellence in medicine. God is not the author of disaster, but He is able to supernaturally turn negative situations around for good. Let's take a look back and see what He's turned around for us.

Our prayer today: Thank You for being my prayer partner. I know that everything I am praying for in the Spirit, under the directions of Holy Spirit, will work for my good. Help me to know, everything that happens to me is happening for me. Open my eyes that I might see the good You are working in others and help them to understand, this is a mere growing process. Heavenly Father I thank You for the healing of Your people and the easing of their pain and suffering. I ask these things in the name of Jesus. Amen

As I wrote about how our words can pollute or purify and this message was brought to light during my husband's surgery this past Thursday. As I sat with him and a member from our church, in what I call the holding pen, there was a lady in the adjoining cube that was anxiously waiting on the arrival of her husband. She had already told the doctor she couldn't go until he got there. A young lady turned the corner, I later learned this was their daughter, and told her he would be late. If I could describe the sound of total helplessness and abandonment, it would be that lady's voice as she told the doctor, "I guess we might as well get this over with." In less than five seconds her husband hastily entered the room, the surgical doors had just closed. He was visibly upset as I heard him tell the nurses at the desk, the elevator had held him up.

I want to feel in my heart their daughter didn't do this intentionally, but I do wonder if she ever once considered the action her words would bring. I started searching for the right scripture, one we can put in our memory bank for future use and I found it in Proverbs 18:20 & 21, *"A man's stomach shall be satisfied from the fruit of his mouth, and from the produce of his lips he shall be filled. Death and life are in the power of the tongue, and those who love it will eat its fruit."* When we stop and think how content we feel when we help someone or put a smile on their face simply by using the right words, then we'll

understand God's plan for us. He is always there holding out His loving arms waiting to give us comfort.

But now the rest of the story. As God would have it, this
lady and my husband were in recovery together. After
her family left I went over to her, talked medical talk for
a few minutes, then I told her how things unfolded, how
her husband had tried to be there and just how devas-
tated he felt. As I started to leave I ask her to try and
keep a positive attitude for the next three weeks while
she was recuperating. I said God loves you and I do too,
I pushed back her hair and kissed her on her forehead.
She reached for my hand and with the most sincerity
I've ever heard, said "thank you."   I truly believe this is
what we're here to do, encourage, listen and help each
other as we pass through this valley. After all God made
two people in the beginning, not one.

Our prayer today: God thank You for giving me the
hope for tomorrow and all mankind, I know with You all
things are possible and help me to always say the right
words of encouragement to others. Hold the sick and
hurting close to Your bosom and ease their pain as we
ask these things in the name of Your Son Jesus. Amen

Philippians 4:11-13, *"Not that I speak in regard to need, for I have learned in whatever state I am, to be content: I know how to abound. Everywhere and in all things I have learned both to be full and to be hungry, both to abound and to suffer need. I can do all things through Christ who strengthens me."*

This passage came to me this morning as I watched different people while waiting at red lights. We were all creating memories on our way to our respective destinations. The majority sipped on their coffee, some were talking to a child strapped in a car seat, yet most were on their cell phones, some seemed angry, others laughing and then there was this man who, I think, was doing the same as me. I noticed him smiling as he was taking this all in and shaking his head in disbelief at the angry people. Which brings me to the question, why are we unhappy when this life is so short and we have much to do for our Lord and families. Most of us take for granted what we already have so we say to ourselves, "I can't enjoy life, I've got too many problems." Right now, today, lets try something new. Lets take an inventory and focus on what we do have, not what we don't have or think we truly need... mainly want. We all have more than we deserve and we still complain.

When was the last time you picked up your toothbrush, looked at it and said "thank You Lord, I can brush my teeth." I remember my #1 son and a group from

his church helping the people after Katrina, he said,
"mom, those people lost everything, they have nothing,
absolutely nothing. They can't even comb their hair,
do you realize how precious a comb is? They sleep on
the ground, yet they don't complain.....seeing this will
humble the strongest of men. Everything they lost, we
take for granted."

Thank God for the blessings you have right now, He really doesn't appreciate an ungrateful or unthankful attitude. It's our choice, so why don't we start today? Let's
make a point of being happy and enjoy life regardless
of the circumstances. When we learn to enjoy this journey we call life and be appreciative, God will give us the
abundant joy He has in store for us. He'll take us places
we can only dream of. So smile at someone, help them
whenever they need help and, let nothing but kind, encouraging words flow from our mouths.

Our prayer today: God, I am so incredibly blessed.
Thank You for all the wonderful things You have given
me. Thank You for having a plan for my life, but most of
all I thank You for loving me unconditionally. Hold the
sick and hurting close and blow Your breath of healing
powers over them as we pray these things in the name of
Your son Jesus. Amen

1 Peter 1:7, *"that the genuineness of your faith, being much more precious than gold that perishes, though it is tested by fire, may be found to praise, honor, and glory at the revelation of Jesus Christ."*

Revelation 21:21, *"And the twelve gates were twelve pearls; each individual gate was of one pearl. And the street of the city was pure gold, like transparent glass."*

I read a story about a miner who struck gold and carried his bag of nuggets with him everywhere. One day he died and went to heaven, still carrying his precious nuggets. When he arrived, an angel asked him why he was carrying asphalt. "

This isn't asphalt", he explained, "it's gold". To which the angel replied, "on earth it's called gold, but here in heaven we use it to pave our street."

Granted, this is just a funny little story, but it makes us stop and think what we consider valuable and what is truly valuable to God. The things we prize here on earth will not be so highly valued in heaven. The unnecessary things we buy and collect, stocks, bank accounts, tangible items and lets not forget, our fame. When the time comes to bid this earth good-bye, what value will "stuff" have?

Read Revelation 21 again, soak in the description of the street, "It's pure gold, like transparent glass" What a sight, this is what we'll be walking on, a precious metal we prize above all metals. We wear it around our necks, let it dangle from our ears, show it off on our fingers, even look at it on our finest dinner wear, and here we are standing on it...WOW....can you imagine, what a reversal! Today, lets start putting value where it really belongs and that's on our relationship with our Heavenly Father.

Our prayer today: Heavenly Father, today I ask You to fill my thoughts with Your thoughts and to fill my heart with Your wisdom. I will choose to focus on You and the good things You have in store for me. Thank You for guiding my every thought and every step. I praise You in the name of Jesus. Amen

Romans 12:16, *"Live in harmony with one another."* *Psalm 32:8, "I will instruct you and teach you."*
So simple yet so powerful. He is the presence of harmony and understanding that blesses all relationships. When we open our eyes, our first words should be, "good morning Lord, thank You for my gift of today", not, "oh good grief, it's Wednesday." By centering our thoughts and feelings on His presence within us, we can get in touch with what's true and genuine, like listening to the news media tell us of the thousands of people throughout the world that didn't receive His gift of today. My prayer is that each of them is walking in the midst of His angels with no pain or fear. Now, get to your feet, stumble to the bathroom, look straight in the mirror and say God loves me....you didn't say it loud enough... point to the mirror, smile and say "GOD LOVES ME." Now doesn't that feel better? I know what's you're thinking, why does He love me, I haven't done anything to deserve it, oh my friend, that's the beautiful part, He loves us unconditionally. We can start today, by putting a smile on our face and letting His light shine through us. We can adopt that winning attitude He gave us from the beginning, we all have choices, let's make the right ones top priority.

Now this brings us to Matthew 18: 21-22, *"Then Peter came to Him and said, Lord, how often shall my brother sin against me and I forgive him? Up to seven times? Jesus said to him, I do say to you, up to seven times, but up to seventy times seven."*

Forgiveness is a daily practice of choosing to avoid harsh judgment and resentment, we are to show love and acceptance. I know for me when I forgive someone of hurtful untruths, I release unwanted hostilities and anguish that would only be a burden and spoil my entire day, which is totally unacceptable, for as I said earlier, this day is special, it's a gift from our Lord. If we would only stop and think how insufficient these things are in the grand scheme of life, then we would see them for what they really are, just a minor inconvenience and not worthy of a second thought. After all, when we refuse to forgive it only hurts us, so the next time someone either intentionally or unintentionally says or does something to hurt you, say "God I forgive them, as You have forgiven me." With a little practice and time we will learn to love ourselves and others as God loves us. What more could we ask for, as a matter of testing ourselves, lets say it one more time...GOD LOVES ME. Just close your eyes and feel the warmth and comfort of His love as it covers your entire being.

We must be on the lookout to share God's mercy and kindness, let's be good to all people. The way we treat others has a great impact on how much of the blessings and favor of God we're going to experience. God will reward our efforts and pour out His abundant blessings on us. As we extend God's mercy to others, we will discover the champion in all of us.

Our prayer today: Heavenly Father, I want to be a pro-active servant of Yours. Please remind me to seek out ways to serve others and to share Your love with all people. Forgive me for putting myself first sometimes and help me to look for ways to share Your love with friends and strangers I encounter today. I ask and accept these things in the name of Jesus. Amen

Psalm 138: 7, *"Though I walk in the midst of trouble, You will revive me; You will stretch out Your hand against the wrath of my enemies, and Your right hand will save me.* 1 Peter 5:10, *But may the God of all grace, who called us to His eternal glory by Christ Jesus, after you have suffered a while, perfect, establish, strengthen, and settle you.*

In this life we will endure struggles and setbacks simply because we believe in our Creator, what He promised from the beginning is still enforce today...A very dear lady sent me a little story I would like to share with you, it so fits our existence as we follow the paths on this journey we call life.

As we all know the Indians, through our history books, folklore and actually talking to them, were a proud people. By proud I mean they stood on their own two feet, made do with what they had or today, have, and never asked or begged for anything. When a young lad was to pass from adolescences to manhood his father would bring him into the forest, blindfold him and leave him there alone. He was required to sit on a stump the entire night and not remove the blindfold until rays of the morning sun shone through. He could not cry out for help to anyone and once he survived the night he was a man. He had to keep this experience to himself, couldn't share with any of the other young boys, because they had to go through this also.

As the young lad sat on the stump and the dark closed in, he began to hear wild animal noises, the wind started to blow and the saw grasses would move up and down his legs and tug gently beneath his feet as if he was in snake infected waters. At times lightening would strike near by and it seemed to him, the earth was shaking the very stump where he sat, but he never once removed the blindfold. Finally, after a horrific night, the morning sun appeared and he removed the cloth from around his face, it was then he discovered his father sitting on the stump next to him. He had been at watch the entire night, protecting his son from harm.

We, too, are never alone. Even when we don't know it, our Heavenly Father is watching, sitting on the stump beside us. When trouble comes, and we know it always does, all we have to do is reach out to Him.

Our prayer today: Heavenly Father, thank You for being so close I can feel Your presence. I can go through my everyday trials knowing I have nothing to fear. I can smile at adversity as if it was never there, because in my heart I know I'm not smiling at the situation, I don't even see it, I see You. Father, today I ask, knowing You are the Great Physician, to guide the hands of the doctors performing surgeries to remove disease and sickness from Your children. I ask these things in the name of Jesus. Amen

1 John 4:18-19, *There is no fear in love; perfect love casts out fear, because fear involves torment. But he who fears has not been made perfect in love. We love Him because He first loved us.*

In today's world it seems every time we listen to our radios, turn on the televisions or read the papers, we are reminded of the cruelty and torment that's around all the time. People are shooting into cars, throwing objects at them, causing wrecks and even death. For no reason you can walk pass someone on a street and get stabbed. This reminds me of the 23rd Psalm verse 4, *Yea, though I walk through the valley of the shadow of death, I will fear no evil; for You are with me; Your rod and Your staff, they comfort me.* Please notice the scripture reads the valley of the shadow of death, not the valley of death. God wants us to rest assured He's our protector.

The children's show host Mister Rogers once said, "love is deep and simple, but what our society gives is shallow and complicated." God's love is perhaps the simplest of all, unconditional, no matter what, He's there waiting to put His arms around us. This kind of love cannot "coexist" with fear. When we discover and really understand the kind of love God has for us, there is no reason left to fear. I know, as well as a lot of you, people who are having surgeries or they're in the hospital, in other words, they're hurting. What we need to remember is God has wonderful and amazing plans for our lives. He will protect us from all evil and bring His purposes for us to pass. These are powerful truths that we can stand on and when we do, fear disappears.

Today, right now, lets say, "thank You Lord for allowing me to see another sunrise, this is a gift from You that I accept with a grateful heart." We should be the happiest people on this earth, we're alive to serve Him one more day, to go about spreading joy and sharing a smile. Do you realize how far a smile can go, trust me on this one, it can go around the world. A smile is like a yawn, it's catching.

Our prayer today: Heavenly Father I will allow no fear, worry, or anxiety to enter my life for any reason. I know You're on my side in every circumstance. You are always for me and never against me, Your love and strength, I hold on to with all my being. Father I ask You to surround the hospitals and mental state of so many with Your angels and allow not one evil disease or thought to enter. We can curb the fears of this world when we allow You to take residence in our hearts. I pray these things in the name of Jesus. Amen

Acts 1:3, *"to whom He also presented Himself alive after His suffer-ing by many infallible proofs, being seen by them during forty days and speaking of the things pertaining to the kingdom of God."*

Has your integrity ever been questioned or compro-mised? It can be a life changing experience and some-times one never gains it back even though they were telling the truth. I'm quiet sure it's the loneliest feeling a person can have, after all, God put us here to comfort each other.

In 1957, Lieutenant David Steeves walked out of the California Sierra Nevada Mountains 54 days after his Air Force trainer jet had disappeared. He told an unbeliev-able tale of how he had live in a snowy wilderness after parachuting from his disabled plane. By the time he showed up alive, he had already been declared officially dead. When search after search failed to turn up the wreckage, a hoax was suspected and Steeves was forced to resign from the Air Force, he was no longer a credit-able citizen to the United States of America. But 20 years later, here comes the Boy Scouts. They were on a camping trip and guess what they found, the remains of the Air Force trainer jet.

Another "survival story" from centuries ago is still con-troversial. A man by the name of Jesus Christ walked out of the Judean wilderness making claims a lot of people found difficult to believe. He was later executed and pronounced dead, but we all know that after three days, He showed up alive. To this day there's still skeptics who will argue this never happened.

But consider the facts of Christ's life, death and resurrection. His integrity is well-founded, prophets foretold of His coming, miracles supported His Supreme Being, eyewitnesses verified His resurrection and yet, to this day, there's still unbelievers. But there's also believers and to us the Holy Spirit confirms the truth, Jesus is alive. When you open your eyes every morning, you see God, when you look in your child's face, or step out of your home, you see God, Just take a 360 degree turn and everywhere you look, there He is, you're looking at the Majesty of our Creator. Although we live in a sinful world, His beauty still surrounds us.

Our prayer today: Thank You Heavenly Father for making me righteous through the blood of Jesus, for turning me from a path of sin and putting my feet on solid ground. Oh, Father, in my deepest thoughts I could never imagine a day without You. My greatest joy is in seeing You everywhere I look, I have to smile at the colorful birds as they fly by, because I know You put them in front of me for my pleasure. Protect the children and elderly of this world from all harm. I ask these things in the name of Jesus. Amen

Psalm 37:21, *"But the righteous shows mercy and gives."* 2
Corinthians 9:7-8, *"So let each one give as he purposes in his
heart, not grudgingly or of necessity; for God loves a cheerful
giver. And God is able to make all grace abound toward you,
that you, always having all sufficiency in all things, may have
an abundance for every good work."*

As this ever growing demand for help approaches us,
lets remember that when we give to others in need, the
Bible says it's like giving directly to God Himself. When
we step out and bless other, we are honoring and blessing our Heavenly Father. Giving is not a decision that
comes from our heads, it comes from the heart, where
the Lord speaks to us.

My husband and I will sometimes stop at Mickey D's
on Sunday morning to grab a quick pick me up before
church, and since the Coca-Cola 600 was in town, we
couldn't get in anywhere else. But, what can I say, we all
know God is in control and He will put you right where
you need to be to do His will. I was in one line and this
elderly gentleman was in the one next to me. He gave
his order and handed the cashier a five dollar bill; she
looked it and was waiting for the remainder. I could
tell it wasn't registering with him. Just then his order
was ready and my brain was working overtime. I asked
my cashier to please tell his, "here's your change." He
took the five and his tray, by this time both cashiers were
looking at me for the money. As I gave her a twenty,

she ask, "do you know him?" No, I told her, it was just something...I looked up at the ceiling...that He wanted me to do. I had to smile as I left with my tray...God has such a sense of humor. A short time later, I went back to get some jelly and the manager asked me where I went to church...what a wonderful opening to invite her.

I believe God has great things in store for us and He will use us daily to make a difference. When we give the best of our ability and are truly eager to give, we can make an impact in our communities and to our close knit groups.

Our prayer today: God, I want to be a cheerful giver. Please help me to always remember that all I have is Yours. I thank You for giving me the ability to share Your Word. Speak to my heart and help me decide what I can give back to You. I ask and receive these things in the name of Jesus. Amen

Psalm 71: 1, 6 & 7, *"In You, O Lord, I put my trust; Let me never be put to shame. (6) By You I have been upheld from my birth; You are He who took me out of my mother's womb. My praise shall be continually of You. (7) I have become a wonder to many, but You are my strong refuge."*

I read a short bio once about a wealthy athlete who built an eight-bedroom home where he lived by himself. His secluded house included a movie theater, a gymnasium, a swimming pool and a five-car garage.

The athlete told The New York Times that he didn't view his $8 million estate as a monument to his success. Instead, he considered it to be a sanctuary from his painful childhood memories of poverty and abuse. The young man was seeking something much deeper than luxury and entertainment. His words were "got to find my peace somewhere."

In today's upside down, seemingly uncaring world, we are all feeling just a little overwhelmed. When the present is daunting and the past is haunting, where can we turn for release and relief? To whom and where do we go for comfort?

The psalmist wrote: *"Deliver me in Your righteousness and cause me to escape; incline Your ear to me and save me. Be my strong refuge to which I may resort continually"* (ps. 71: 2-3). This athlete, now growing older, proved to himself and the world, he could be somebody, but the greatest blessing came when he realized how empty he still felt and got down on his knees. God was his hope, his trust and his hiding place in the storms of life. He said, " while my mansion stands stately as always, I now see stuff. I've got my eyes fixed on a higher prize."

E. May Grimes wrote a poem while standing at Mount Watkins, looking down at Mirror Lake in Yosemite National Park which is so fitting in our troubled lives today. "A little sanctuary art Thou to Me; O Jesus Christ, beloved, I live with Thee; My heart has found its everlasting home, Its sure abiding place where'er I roam." He looked and saw God; we can do the same thing. All we have to do is open our eyes, He's everywhere.

Our prayer today: Father God help us to see what's really important today. Although we may lose our jobs, homes, or even retirement, nothing compares to what You have in store for us. May we always remember we're to store our treasures in heaven, not here on earth. Father God, I know I ask this of You everyday, I think it's because the children and helpless elderly of this world can't help themselves. Please keep the wall of angels around them. Keep them safe from all harm and fed until the day we all look upon Your face. I ask this in the name of Jesus. Amen.

Luke 3: 14-16...*"Do not intimidate anyone or accuse falsely, and be content with your wages. " Now as the people were in expectation, and all reasoned in their hearts about John, whether he was the Christ or not, John answered, saying to them all, "I indeed baptize you with water; but One mightier than I is coming, whose sandal strap I am not worthy to loose. He will baptize you with Holy Spirit and with fire. "*

How many times have you heard or said yourself, "don't blame me, I'm just the messenger." Dave Thomas, founder of Wendy's restaurants appeared in most of his own commercials. As a matter of fact, he appeared in more commercials than anyone before him or since, a total of 800. His viewers saw him as friendly, funny, believable and caring. He never forgot his humble beginnings for as an infant he was adopted by a construction worker and his wife. At the old age of 15 he struck out on his own, and by 35 he was a millionaire. He eventually opened 6000 restaurants with an annual revenue of $6 billion, not bad for a child born of a single, poverty stricken mom, But In spite of his popularity, Thomas always said he was "the messenger, not the message." He said God was with him all the time and he never thought about his fortune. He just wanted people to know, through it all, they had someone who cared.

This is good to remember as we speak about Christ to our friends and family. While our behavior should always be consistent with what we say, our goal is to point others to Jesus and not to ourselves. Like last week when we were reminded that our walk speaks louder than our talk, as God's messengers we must always put our best foot forward. To prove we are the messengers look at 2 Corinthians 4:5, *"For we do not preach ourselves, but Jesus Christ the Lord."* We're to let others know we care and we want to share our Heavenly Fathers love with them.

John the Baptist knew that his role was to be a messenger for Christ. When people flocked to hear John preach and to be baptized, a sign of their repentance, many wondered if he was the promised Messiah, John told them, "I indeed baptize you with water; but One mightier than I is coming, whose sandal strap I am not worthy to loose." Through our words and actions, we testify of Jesus Christ as Savior and Lord. We are indeed the messengers; He is the message. A good quote to remember is, "We witness best for Christ when we say the least about ourselves."

Our prayer today: Thank you Heavenly Father for always being at my side, You stay so close I can actually feel your presence and I praise You for this. Remind me to walk the walk of faith so others might see and desire Your favor. I ask and receive these things in the name of Jesus. Amen.

Ephesians 4:31-32, *"Let all bitterness, wrath, anger, clamor and evil speaking be put away from you, with all malice. And be kind to one another, tender-hearted, forgiving one another, just a God in Christ also forgave you. "*

James 4:11 *"Do not speak evil of one another, brethren. "*

Mark 11:25-25 *"And whenever you stand praying, if you have anything against anyone, forgive him, that your Father in heaven may also forgive you your trespasses. But if you do not forgive, neither will your Father in heaven forgive your trespasses. "*

How many times has someone really hurt you, the kind of hurt, as some would say, I'll take this to my grave. The hurt that keeps raising it's ugly head. Every time you hear the persons' name or see something that reminds you of them, there it is. The pain just won't go away. It's like a sore that scabs over only to fester again and again. You tell yourself, you forgave them, but hear the news of something bad happening to them and the first words from your mouth, they got just what they deserved," or "it couldn't have happened to a nicer person." Forgiveness is an unnatural act and is achingly difficult. Long after you've forgiven, the wound lives on in memory.

Not forgiving can cause us hypertension, heart disease, sleepless nights, loss of appetite or overeating and now, I recently heard the stress levels may actually cause cancer. I think this sums it up so well. Corrie Ten Boom, a Christian woman who survived a Nazi concentration camp during the Holocaust said, "forgiveness is to set a prisoner free, and to realize the prisoner was you."

We will know the work of forgiveness is complete when we experience the freedom that comes as a result. We are the ones who suffer most when we choose not to forgive. When we do forgive, the Lord sets our heart free from the anger, bitterness, resentment and hurt that previously imprisoned us. He died on a rugged cross for our sins, can't we just let go of our vindictiveness against each other?

Our prayer today: Father in heaven, thank You for sending Your Son, Jesus, to show me the way. I invite You into every area of my life. Help me to always forgive the ones who trespass against me, just as you forgive my trespasses. May my light always shine toward others for Your name sake. I ask these things in the name of Jesus. Amen.

Psalm 138: 3 & 7, *In the day when I cried out, You answered me, and made me bold with strength in my soul. Though I walk in the midst of trouble, you will revive me; You will stretch out Your hand against the wrath of my enemies, and Your right hand will save me.*

When our children were reaching leaving the nest age, I asked my husband what were we going to do when a way of life we had known for over twenty five years, would be over. This was a frightening time for me, and I know a lot of you can identify with this; if you're not there yet, you will be one day. I had heard of many people getting divorced or simply growing apart. We had worked hard preparing our children to stand on their own two feet; this consumed our lives. Their dad would always tell them, when you have a problem ask yourself first, what would I do if my dad and mom were no longer here, then come to us. But, being the mom, I wanted them to know as long as we had a home, they would always have a safe haven where they could come and escape from the world. Our number three son asked me one day, "Mom, how long can I live at home;" I told him he couldn't stay here and draw social security. Although I knew he didn't understand, he smiled as though he did. Feeling very inadequate and fearful, secretly I worried, "did we do everything right, have we really taught them how to survive on their own." To put it mildly, I was a wreck, the "woe is me" syndrome.

I have a sister-in-law who knew I had always put God first, but one day, I guess she could see I was struggling. She said to me, put God in the middle, so whatever direction you reach, there He is. I thought what a simple idea, make a circle of your life, then right in the middle of it all, put our Heavenly Father.

In Psalm 34:19, *"A Righteous man may have many troubles, but the Lord delivers him from them all."* No matter what "troubles" we may be facing today, God has promised to deliver us! Notice the verse doesn't say He's going to deliver us from "some" of our troubles if we say and do everything perfectly. No, if we are righteous today, God promises to deliver us from "all" of our troubles. When we accept His forgiveness and believe He is working in our life, then we are righteous. Our faith and belief in the goodness of our God is His righteousness at work in our hearts.

I quickly learned I don't always need miracles; sometimes I just need a minor lifestyle change. If you are in that place in life where you are going through the routines of the day, but your life isn't really going where you want it to go, you may need a minor lifestyle shift also. Not a miraculous wonder, but an adjustment that will put you where God wants you to be. As for my children leaving home, our Father worked that out just perfectly, there again, I call them God winks. The last one left at home, in his senior year, decided to work part-time at

KFC. I learned dinner didn't have to be on the table at a certain time, the phone wasn't ringing off the hook (before cell phones) and I had at least four free hours a night. I could take long walks, even go shopping and not have to be in a hurry. Life was good, thank You God.

Our prayer today: Jesus, I receive Your promises and choose to believe that You are always working behind the scenes on my behalf. Thank You for being my Deliverer today and everyday. Heavenly Father please show me if I need a lifestyle change to get on tract with You. Guide me today as I seek your wisdom and strength. I ask and receive these things in the name of Jesus. Amen

1 Peter 5: 6 & 7, *"Therefore humble yourselves under the mighty hand of God, that He may exalt you in due time, casting all your care upon Him, for He cares for you."*

How many times have you worked at gathering material for a special message you were to deliver or prepared yourself to entertain a large group just to realize the words weren't coming out the way you planned, such is the case for me. I thought I knew exactly what I was going to write about today, but this morning as I was going about my morning routine, and praising our Heavenly Father, it was if He said, *"forget what you think is best and type the words I give you, I'm your Father and I know best."* I keep saying He has a great sense of humor.   I can just see a smile on His wonderful face as He made the skunk, with a beautiful fur coat of black with perfect white stripes and a smell "whew" Lysol can't remove.

We all have our cross to bear, but we don't have to carry the load. Lets think of our Heavenly Father as our earthly parent. He's here to protect, love, discipline and teach us as we teach our children. We want the very best for ours and so does He. When we stop and look at the big picture, He made the universe, something to keep us intrigued for a life time, hence the phrase, an idle mind is the devils workshop. He doesn't want our minds to be empty, we're to always keep our focus on Him. We want to think, or sometimes I wonder if we really do, that this earth, with all it's beauty, is suppose to be here, but take another look. What we call wild flowers is actually the ones God put here, He gave man the knowledge to cross pollinate creating the hybrids we have today. While most of us admire and appreciate the fields and roadsides of endless color , others would rather mow them down. Right now, the Queen Anne's Lace is blooming everywhere you look, stop along the road and pick one. Look at the mass of tiny petals all placed in perfect form to look just like lace and then say to yourself, "I am looking at the handy work of our Almighty God."

This is pretty much what He wanted me to say, *"Look at me, I'm everywhere and I love you. Take my hand and lets walk for awhile together."*

Our prayer today: Father in Heaven, I receive Your Word into my heart today. Thank You for choosing me so that I can be a blessing to others. Show me ways to bless others and teach me to receive all You have for me. I ask these things in the name of Jesus. Amen

Genesis 2: 7, *"And the Lord God formed man of the dust of the ground, and breathed into his nostrils the breath of life; and man became a living being."*

Jeremiah 1:5, "Before I formed you in the womb I knew you."

Matthew 25:35, "For I was hungry and you gave Me food; I was thirsty and you gave Me drink; I was a stranger and you took Me in."

As I was having my quiet time with our Savior this morning, for some unknown reason, I lifted my head and when I opened my eyes, there in front of me was the sculpture of Jesus' hands my oldest son had given me many years ago. For some reason my attention was fixed on those hands and I started to reflect on just some of the above scriptures. The first words in the book of Genesis, say *"God created the heavens and the earth,"* simply by speaking what He wanted done; but in the second chapter He used His hands to form man and woman.

I remember shortly before my husband's demise, in a tender voice barely audible, he asked me to take his hand. He tried to talk but he was too tired. As I held his thin, wrinkled hand I looked back over the years we had shared, the things he had done, all because God gave him two good hands. His lips formed a faint smile as I reminded him of all he had done passing through on this journey we call life. "It's been good and I praise my God." he whispered.

Let's take a moment and really look at our hands. If you're like me, you take them for granted. Our hands are tools; we use them to feed ourselves, tend our gardens, fix motors and put clothes on our backs. They're weapons; we use them to protect ourselves as well as our families and they're pain relievers; we use our hand to simply touch others which erases pain and fear.

Now let's think about our Heavenly Father, and all His hands have done for us. We have no fear because we know He is our strength, we never feel alone, because He is always everywhere waiting for us to take His hand. Sometimes I look up and say, "Lord, can I take Your hand and let's just walk awhile?"   Before long everything looks a lot better and I'm right with the world again. All it takes is His gentle touch.

Our prayer today: Father, thank You for giving me my hands to help guide and heal as I go through this journey, walking to the other side. Sometimes, I have to just sit and remember your words in Psalms 46:10, *"Be still, and know that I am God."* This brings so much peace to me. I pray and offer thanks for loving me. Amen

Proverbs 16:9, *"A man's heart plans his way, But the Lord directs his steps."*

Philippians 3:13-14, *"Brethren, I do not count myself to have apprehended; but one thing I do, forgetting those things which are behind and reaching forward to those things which are ahead, I press toward the goal for the prize of the upward call of God in Christ Jesus."*

We all wish for many good things, but not too many of us see those good things happen in our lives. Most of us don't know the difference between a wish and a goal.

A goal is something realistic and something we can achieve. I could wish all day to become an airline pilot, but that could never be a goal for me because I'm afraid of heights. A goal has a time frame and is something you can measure. I may wish to lose weight, but in order to do that, I need to set a goal and time frame. "I will lose ten pounds in one month." That's a realistic goal.

We may wish for a closer walk with God; get to know the Bible better, or learn how to pray with power. These are good wishes and are achievable, but only if we turn them into goals. For us to obtain our goals, we must also have a set of plans. Something tangible on paper we can look at each day. This keeps us on track, we know where we've been and how far we have to go. A goal I have set for myself is to have a conversation each morning with God and to make sure my family knows how much I truly love them.

Our prayer today: Thank You Father God for setting before us the ultimate prize and giving us the goals to reach it. You gave us Your set of plans in the Bible for us to refer to daily. Give us the knowledge to realize, what seems as impossible, is possible. We ask and accept these truths in the name of Jesus. Amen.

Psalm 127:3 & 4, *Behold, children are a heritage from the Lord. Like arrows in the hand of a warrior, so are the children of one's youth.*

Proverbs 20:7, *The righteous man walks in his integrity; His children are blessed after him.*

On a bright sunny Saturday, a grown man of 45 years of age, called his mother to ask, "what am I going to do in the morning, I'm always the first one to call dad and wish him a Happy Father's day?" The mother thought for a minute, "son, just take a deep breath, look toward heaven and tell him, he'll hear you." "But I can't see him," he said in a broken voice. "While this is true, he sees you, and he's still watching over you just like when you were a little boy." The mom proceeded to tell the story she knew he loved so much about when he was very small and he only saw his dad on the weekends. He was asleep when his dad went to work and in bed when he arrived home after a long day. The first thing he did every morning and night was to gently ease the bedroom door open and check on him; he couldn't see him then either but he was there.

As his dad grew older and finally retired he was truly sorry he didn't adjust his work schedule and spend more, needed quality time with him. Like he said, my job would have filled my position overnight but my family will feel the loss for the rest of their lives. It's true, wisdom comes with age. This is the reason you hear so many grandparents tell their adult children, don't exhaust yourselves with rising early and going to bed late, busying yourselves to make your mark on the world, all the while overlooking the one investment that matters beyond everything else, your children. We live on through the smiles, eyes and integrity of our children.

This reminded me of Hebrews 13:5, *"I will never leave you nor forsake you."* Our Heavenly Father is always watching over and taking care of us just like our earthly fathers. So let's make time for our children and trust that the Lord will provide for all of our physical needs. Children, whether our own or those we come in contact with, are our lasting legacy.

Our prayer today: Father God, thank You for the gift of my children and the habits of honesty and love for their fellow man their earthly father instilled in them. Your gift to us made our lives complete and we could never praise You enough for it. Help me to teach my children how to stay on the right road and for them to always seek Your guidance in absolutely everything. I ask these things in the name of Your Son, Jesus. Amen.

Matthew 21:13, *"It is written"* he said to them, *"My house will be called a house of prayer, but you are making it a den of robbers. "*

As I was asking God for our message and waiting for His answer, the Commandment, *"You shall not steal"* kept entering my thought process, I knew this was from Him, because He talks in a soft voice. I've never heard anyone say, "God yelled at me." He may get our attention in a strong way, but He's soft spoken with His children.

Exodus 20:15 *"You shall not steal"*, means more than just material things. We can take what isn't ours while no one is looking or we can use a gun or knife to rob since this is a coward's way of life. These people not only take material things, they also rob us of our self esteem and the security of who we are as an adult. We also steal, or let me put it this way, we misuse things which don't belong to us. Concerning our employ, do we always come to work on time, do we stay our scheduled time? Do you take the pen you were using and bring it home or a half used pad of post it notes? Do you use the office phone for long distance personal calls? Would we scroll the internet with the same content if our supervisor or boss was watching? Do we speak rude to others, robbing them of their joy? Do we make people think one way, when it's really another. There's so many ways to go against the commandment of God other than the obvious. What we should remember is there's no gray area with Him, it's either right or wrong. His word says, He'd rather have us cold than lukewarm.

I can still see a little girls face beaming with pride as she runs to her mother to give her a fresh flower she had just picked, the mother looked down at her and said you better not have gotten that from my prize bush. She stole this child's joy and self esteem when all she was really giving, was her heart. We need to think sometimes before we react.

Our prayer today, Dear Lord, thank You for giving me a mouth, but I pray, help me to use it wisely. May I always practice Your ways and be a witness for You. God, please give the sick and hurting Your loving touch today and assure them You're there. Amen

Genesis 1:1-31 & 2:1, *"In the beginning God created the heavens and the earth." "Then God saw everything that He had made and indeed it was very good." "Thus the heavens and the earth and all the host of them were finished."*
Malachi 3:6, *"For I am the Lord, I do not change."*
Isaiah 11:9, *"They shall not hurt nor destroy in all My holy mountain."*
Hebrews 13:8, *"Jesus Christ is the same yesterday, today and forever."*

In today's trying times we see people being consumed with the demands of the world, feeling as though they are all alone, a figure in the middle of a vast ocean going down for the last time. Gloom and doom, this is what we hear if we listen to the news media We need to remember, the script writers are paid a huge sum of money to win over the majority of the audience. The media decides if the stock market is up or down, what cars are the best buy, who we elect to the political fields, what medicine will help us, the housing crunch, even down to what we wear. Aren't we glad we have a Savior who doesn't care about stuff, His primary concern is us and our happiness.

My brother is here from New Jersey and he told me of a sign he saw on a church billboard, "under the same management for the last 2000 years." God is not in the real estate business, He planned and made our earthly home from scratch with His own hands, and it has never been for sale. It makes me happy to know I don't have to worry about who might be my new landlord.

What other landlord do you think would wake you each morning with the light of the sun, command the birds to sing sweet songs for your ears, and place fresh flowers everywhere for your eyes to feast upon? We don't have to worry about Him changing His mind and telling us to get out, He's the same yesterday, today and forever.

Maybe we can help others realize, this is not the end; this is the beginning of a new relationship with our Creator. He's all we will ever need. Every opportunity we have lets try to offer a kind word of encouragement, even if we're in the waiting room at the doctor's office. Just think, that may be the only word of encouragement they receive all day! Remember God has you there for a reason! Love your neighbor, even the slow ones, as Christ loves us. Be flexible in these times and learn to go with the flow. When you do, our Heavenly Father will begin to show you more peace, more of His joy and more of the victory He has in store for you.

Our prayer today: God, thank You for allowing me to open my eyes this morning to see Your goodness and beauty. Help me to always remember You will never change and my life is in Your hands. You will keep my feet on the steady path as I continue on this journey we call life. When I am tempted to stew or complain, I will look instead for the reason I am in this situation and use it to Your glory. We ask and accept these things in the name of Jesus. Amen.

Most of us know when the Lord tells you to do something, He means it. For the last month it has been on my mind so strong to write about the tenth commandment and I could never find the right opening. Each week I would ask, "Lord use me to deliver Your message, what pleases You today?" I received the same answer as the week before, the tenth commandment. Our God, being the teacher that He is decided one night for me to get confused thinking I was on the HGTV channel when I was actually on the one just before it. Now you say how can you get that mixed up? Well the couple on the show was hosting a dinner party and everyone was commenting on how nice the house looked with all the renovations, so naturally I didn't think anything of it until I saw a dirty pair of shoes standing in a dark corner of the back deck. I thought to myself, what's this? Then I saw that same pair of shoes enter through the unlocked back door and while everyone was leaving, this intruder, picked up the receiver and dialed 911. He told the operator there was going to be two people murdered and when she ask why, he told her, they have things I want. Bingo, thank you Lord for my answer. He's breaking the tenth commandment and by breaking this one, it's causing him to break three more, he doesn't love his neighbor as himself, he's going to kill two innocent people and he is taking things that were never his.

"You shall not covet your neighbor's house; you shall not covet your neighbor's wife, nor his male servant, nor his female

servant, nor his ox, nor his donkey, nor anything that is your neighbor's," Exodus 20:17 Unlike the other nine, this is where satan works the hardest, if he can convince us what we feel is actually right in our minds, then he's won and the only way we can defeat covetousness is through our relationship with God. It's perfectly okay to be happy for someone who has a nicer house than you and to let them know it, but then, don't go to another neighbor and say harsh words about them. Oh, I know you've heard it and seen it, a person will come to you and say, "they think they're something with that big new house, manicured lawn and just where did they get the money to buy that automobile, (this is one step up from a car), they think they're so hot." Does this sound familiar? Oh, yes, we've all heard it from time to time. We've also heard, "look what I just bought, I worked hard all my life, I deserve it, no one helped me, no sir, I got this on my own." This is called selfish ambition and not from our Lord at all.

Now let's get to the coveting wife part or in today's society we must also include the husband. I have often wondered if a person really stops and thinks about the consequence of adultery or fornication. The broken homes, fatherless or motherless mornings, children looking around with yearning and hopelessness in their eyes. Dinner tables with less than enough food or maybe no dinner at all. Let's also take into consideration the percentage of homeless mothers and children, where the shelters are full; they resort to sleeping in the woods or under bridges. Now I don't know about you, but this really disturbs me. We sit in our churches and homes, we talk about the state of our young people, the needs of our young people, what to do with our young people, need I go on? It's time to start taking steps to teach our young not to do as some of their parents or mentors has, this vicious tread can be reversed. We must teach our children that sex outside of marriage is not the norm nor is it permissible under the direction of our Lord, that drugs and alcohol is a weapon the devil uses to drag them down with him; however, he's the only one that enjoys the landing.

Our prayer today: Lord, help us to always teach our children the ten commandments and to live our lives in such a way they will see them demonstrated each day. Please hold the sick and hurting in your tender arms and ease their pain....we ask this in the name of Your son Jesus...Amen

M . E L A I N E   E L R O D

Each day of my life and everything that happens in that day is absolutely amazing to me. One of our sons and his family came this past weekend for the Bank of America 500 race at Lowe's Motor Speedway. While I was on a natural high Friday and Saturday, Sunday when they pulled out, I hit an all time low. One where my heart was dissolving, oozing into the concrete which is called our driveway. You mothers and fathers know exactly what I'm talking about here, tears large enough to take a bath in. I went back in the house, pulled a chair from the dining table and thought, I have earned this moment so I'll just sit here and feel sorry for myself. But the Lord had different plans for me. I heard His tender, soft voice and felt His touch as He said *"seize this day, live in the now."* Don't live in the past or future, but consciously live in the now moment, every day. When we shift our thinking to the present, we discover an endless stream of blessings and opportunities. Jesus himself lived in the now and He encourages us to do the same. The mountains are my place of renewal, so my husband and I took a little trip north. I found myself thanking Him for giving me my eyes to see all His awesome wonder and suddenly I was praising Him for giving me my family....I was living in the now.

In John 4:35 He said to His disciples, *"Do you not say, There are still four months and then comes the harvest? Behold, I say to you, lift up your eyes and look at the fields, for they are already white for harvest.* And in Matthew 9:37,

He said to His disciples, *"The harvest truly is plentiful, but the laborers are few."* All we need to do is live in the now, be thankful for "this" day, rejoice in it. Everyday, get up expecting good news, when you meet a friend or co-worker ask them, "what are you expecting God to do for you today?" They may look at you as if you've lost your mind, but that's okay, they are thinking. As we think, so we are, this is the spiritual law of cause and effect. Our thoughts take form in our lives and isn't it wonderful to know we can change our thought process. Let's seize the day and every "now" opportunity to change our thinking and our lives, let's be the way we know we should be.

Our prayer today: Lord, thank You for all Your healing powers bestowed on four of Your children I know, You freed their bodies of cancer and I humbly praise Your name in grateful gratitude. Lord, I pray, continue to place Your loving touch on the sick and hurting, give them peace. In Jesus name, Amen.

1 Thessalonians 2:19, *For what is our hope, or joy, or crown of rejoicing? Is it not even you in the presence of our Lord Jesus Christ at His coming?*

Daniels 12:3, *Those who are wise shall shine like the brightness of the firmament, and those who turn many to righteousness, like the stars forever and ever.*

I saw a sign in front of a church which read, "Your walk is louder than your talk" and I thought back to an incident which happened a number of years ago. I was a realtor selling a house to a pastor and his wife from another state. They both had very expensive taste, which was alright, but they wanted it for a small sum. Immediately I thought, why are you degrading everyone's home and furnishings when all you would have to say is, "this isn't exactly what we're looking for." Neither one ever said anything specific, but their attitude spoke volumes. His demeanor was worse than hers and when another realtor asked me, "isn't he a pastor," I thought what am I supposed to say? I didn't want to say anything negative, but I couldn't hide the truth either. I merely replied, they're in a strange state and I think they're a little nervous. Secretly I was troubled over the fact of how he would treat his congregation, but apparently he was totally different in the house of our Father or maybe he saw his reflection in the mirror and decided it was time for a change. He was still there the last time I heard from them.

You and I can be sure that our Lord God is with us wherever we go, and He knows everything that happens to us. As the all-powerful One, He is able to solve every problem, no matter how overwhelming or perplexing it may be, We are never alone, never forgotten, and never beyond hope and I find this so comforting.

Whatever is troubling us, whether we're afflicted by illness or injury, brokenhearted over the loss of a loved one, disillusioned because our dearest friend has betrayed or rejected us, God knows and cares. We may be deeply depressed, or perhaps we're plagued by loneliness and discouragement; it doesn't matter, we can always be confident that we are under His watchful eye. Whatever we do, lets make sure our walk and talk will encourage someone to want what we have. I, like you, keep my eyes looking toward heaven because I know one day I will look into the face of our Father. I don't know exactly how I will react, but every time I think about it, I get this big smile on my face. How about you?

Our prayer today: Father, teach and help me to always walk and talk in such a way, it will be encouraging to others. Always keep me mindful of my actions. I thank You for Your ever presence in my life, the security and warmth I feel knowing You are there. I pray hold the sick and hurting so close their pain will be gone forever. In Jesus name. Amen.

Each day when I get home, I have a set routine, I'm like a robot, I know exactly where to go or turn and very rarely do I vary from it, because if I do, it throws everything out of whack and I'm going to forget to do something. Are you like this? When I think most everything is done and my body is screaming from fatigue, I take a deep breath and I go to my quite corner. This is where I stop fussing and fretting, I release all my anxieties and concerns about everything, everyone and myself. Please, if you don't already have this place, find one and let God take care of the daily circumstances in your life. When we know within ourselves, *God is taking care of it*, we will realize we can let go and feel a sense of relief and just relax. He's dissolving whatever needs dissolving and resolving whatever needs resolving. Sometimes we're afraid of what might happen next week, next month or even next year, remember again, *God is taking care of it.*

As you sit there and totally relax in God's presence, you will find yourself thinking more clearly and sleeping more restful. Sometimes I have to smile when I'm rehearsing the events of the day; the mountain I thought was in front of me was a mere stepping stone. Psalm 23:2 *"He leads me beside still waters"*, Psalm 4:4, *"Commune with your own heart...and be silent."* and Psalm 4:8, *"I will both lie down and sleep in peace."* There in the stillness is where the blessings of God begins, for in the stillness is God, the giver of all good things. Jesus said in Luke 17:21 *"the kingdom of God is in the midst of you"*. The things of this world will not bring us peace, no matter how much we accumulate, but we can find it when we get quiet... with God, and we need this time, it makes us better people. Have you noticed when you've had a restful night, your muscles aren't tied in knots and the acid reflux is gone, people look better and they seem nicer....or...maybe we're nicer. Could it be we harvest what we sow? I've noticed most people will smile and speak when they're greeted in the same manner. Wouldn't it be wonderful if in the whole world, just one day, everybody had a smile on their face? For this one day, there would be no child or spousal abuse, no killings, suicides, robberies or bad words spoken, tearing down of ones' life.

Our prayer today: Thank you God for creating and loving us unconditionally, we're Your children and You, our Father. We rest in the peace knowing You know our concerns and needs before we do and You have everything under control. Cradle the sick and hurting so that they may feel Your warmth. We ask these things knowing they will be done...Amen

I was reading the news on the internet yesterday and I was slapped in the face with the reality, this year is gone. It stated this was the last full moon for the year and I thought where this year has gone or better yet where have I been. My dad used to joke about when you're young, time seems to drag, but you hit forty it speeds up and before you know it, you're fifty and you're on a whirly bird. Back then I didn't understand what he was trying to tell me but I certainly do now. He also had another saying, slow down, take a deep breath, smell the air, you can tell a lot about a day by the smell of the air; I can't, but then he was half Cherokee Indian. I have learned to slow down because as individuals we earnestly desire peace, young or old. We desire peace in our homes, our workplace, our country and our relationships with one another. Deep down I think we all believe what the angels said heralding the birth of Jesus saying *"On earth peace."* The scripture actually reads in Luke 2:14, *"Glory to God in the highest, and on earth peace, good will toward men!"* Also in John 14:27, *"Peace I leave with you, My peace I give to you; not as the world gives do I give to you."* We think we can buy enough things or surround ourselves with enough people to make the world go away, it's not going to happen.

To truly be happy and have peace, try giving your life away and before you know it, the blessings of God will chase you and overtake you. If you don't believe this is true, ask me. I know people who have a smile on their face every time you meet them and I'm sure they're just like us. They have daily problems, but they take them with the same attitude they live by, God is in control. We've all got plenty to give, a smile, a kind word or simply time. A smile is contagious, a kind word can boost ones' self esteem and time is the most precious commodity we have. We can comfort someone who is hurting, we can let people who only have a couple of items get in front of us in the checkout line. How many times have we made funny faces at children just to keep them quiet while their mothers unloaded a shopping cart? Begin each day with a determination to be a blessing to as many people as possible. We will be so blessed we won't be able to contain it.

Our prayer today, Thank you God for thinking of me first. Give me the strength and the thoughtfulness to see the needs of others. I lift up to You the sick and hurting knowing with You all things are possible, I have seen Your healing works, I have seen sadness turn to joy and tears brought to a stop. Bless Your Holy Name.... Amen

Have you ever had a day when there should have been more of you? This way you could get everything accomplished before the sun went down and some of us don't stop even then. The old saying, "a man's work is from sun to sun, but a woman's work is never done", is not entirely true in today's world. With all the modern conveniences, we're working longer and burning up the micro chips in our brains, both male and female species. Sometimes I look up and say dear God, where's the sanity? And I know I'm not alone doing this, I've seen the looks of despair on many faces, then Psalm 46:10 rings in my ears, *"Be still and know that I am God"*. Psalm 124:8 also says, *"Our help is in the name of the Lord, Who made heaven and earth"*. If we can always remember yesterday is history, tomorrow is a mystery and today is a gift, then we will slow down for just a few minutes and soak it all in. There's a reason we woke up this morning and it wasn't because of the alarm clock, baby or the dog. It was our gift from Him. He has something planned for our lives and knowing God, it's something good, something we should get excited about, we should put a smile on our face knowing we're already a winner.

Lets consider the day in Jesus' life, one of which is written in Mark 1:21-34. He started His day teaching at the synagogue when a demon-possessed man began shouting at Him, He calmly walked over to the man, cast out the demon and went back to work. When His work day was over, He and some of His friends went to Peter's house, but He couldn't rest because Peter's mother-in-law was sick and needed His healing touch. He did heal her and we know how fast good news can travel, when He went to leave, all the sick in the town had gathered outside Peter's house waiting to be healed. The scripture doesn't tell us what time Jesus got home that night, but it does tell us, He didn't take the next day off, in v.35, He got up before sunrise, found a solitary place, and prayed. He sought the rejuvenating power of His Father's presence. This is how we need to start our day, get alone somewhere with God and seek His help.

When you feel the tension mounting, and across the busy day only gloomy clouds are drifting, as you start to worry—pray! If you're too busy to pray, you're too busy.

Our prayer today: Thank You dear God for bringing us back to reality, only Your love for us matters. Help us to remember when we're trapped in the snare to seek You first and watch as Your nail-pierced hands opens it up and sets us free. We pray today for a miracle, for You to remind the surgeons they're merely robots, You're the great physician as You heal the bodies of many. Wrap the sick and hurting in Your loving arms and ease their pain....we ask these things, knowing they will be done, in the name of Jesus...Amen.

A Special Gift

To my dismay this past weekend, I heard a radio station playing Christmas carols and I said to my husband, I can't believe this, is this some kind of a promotion? He looked at me with an expression like where have you been and said well Thanksgiving is a week from Thursday and then four weeks to Christmas. WWWWWHAT??????, heart don't fail me now. Come on world, stop.... and let me catch up. I started thinking back, covering each month, as though it had passed without me knowing it. I kept repeating, what.. have... I... done... this... year? I became a little concerned as I thought about the scripture in the book of John that says "*I am the true vine, and My Father is the vinedresser. Every branch in Me that does not bear fruit He takes away; and every branch that bears fruit He prunes, that it may bear more fruit.*", so I decided until the end of this year, each and everyday, after dinner, I'm going to my quite place and write down four things that happened during the day, good, bad or indifferent.

I picked only four things, although our days are packed with many happenings, because I think we can address these without it taking the rest of the night. By each item I write down, I'm asking myself what could I have done differently, am I satisfied with the results as they are, did I act with God's spirit in my heart. You see we all need pruning sometimes, but I don't want Him to get out the saw. By analogizing the functions of our day, if we do see where we could have handled something a little better, we will ace it the next time. After all, people can't see God in the flesh, but they can see Him in us. As we think about all the things we have to be thankful for this Thanksgiving, lets please remember our forefathers who came to this country in search of religious freedom. A country where we are free to live our lives as we see fit, although we might not understand how some could possibly be happy living theirs as they do, it's their right. We can only do God's will and let our light shine.

I would like to send you a special thanksgiving prayer... my prayer is God will pour out His blessings on you because I know you're so deserving, I pray He will keep you pruned so you will bear much fruit and share your knowledge and bounty with others. May His light always shine in and through you...May you have good health and be satisfied with who you are...in Jesus name, Amen.

I've tried so hard to come up with something festive since this is close to Christmas, however, hard as I try, God keeps reminding me why we have an extra spring in our step, song on our lips, and smile on our face. It's all because of His love. Despite our efforts to keep Him out, God intrudes. He loves us so much He entered our world through a door marked No Entrance and left through a door marked No Exit. I have actually sat in my "quiet" chair and tried to think of words that would describe this kind of love, my mind can't comprehend it. To me the greatest love we have is for our children, I try to compare this with His but I can't, because when my little angels puck my last nerve all that comes to me is the saying I have used and I hope you have, I wouldn't want to be the only one, I brought you in this world, I'll take you out. When we commit an unthinkable sin, God is standing there with His arms outstretched waiting to hold us, maybe we should try this also.

Deuteronomy 6:5-7, *"You shall love the Lord your God with all your heart, with all your soul and with your might. Write these words that I've given you today on your hearts. Get them inside of you and then get them inside your children. Talk about them wherever you are, sitting at home or walking in the street; talk about them from the time you get up in the morning to when you fall into bed at night.* He saw our needs from heaven so He filled the stable in Bethlehem and the cross of Calvary, He didn't wait for an invitation; He knew what was going to happen to Him, and still He came, yet, all He commands of us is love. His definition of love won't be found in Webster's dictionary or our memory banks. It's His first commandment, our road map for living with ourselves and others. If there's one thing we should remember it's, God lived as our teacher, died as our sacrifice and rose from the grave as our Savior. Christmas is coming.....and so is Easter.

Our prayer today: God, thank You for giving me Your word, I do love You with all my heart and I strive each day to let Your love show through me, it's a wonderful, comforting feeling. Precious Lord, I pray ease the pain of the sick and hurting, let them touch the hem of Your garment and be healed. I pray this in the name of Your Son Jesus....Amen

Matthew 2:11 *"On coming to the house, they saw the child with his mother Mary, and they bowed down to worship Him. Then they opened their treasures and presented Him gifts: gold, frankincense, and myrrh.*

Christmas is just around the corner and with each message I feel as though we're in our special room having a private conservation. Most of us have never met or spoken to each other, yet there's a kinship, if you will, a closeness. We've never seen our Lord, but we know He's there for us to call on, just like we should feel comfortable reaching out to one another.

I would like to share a true story with you today, some have already read it; but in this fall season when the air has a cold nip to the nose, the trees and plants are covered in their coats of many colors, stores and homes are decorated with the finest of care and everyone scurries about with great expectancy on their faces, this one covers the true meaning why God sent His son Jesus to show us the way.

This lady works with Publix in Tallahassee Florida and was so moved by the actions of a stranger, she sent this to me.

The story starts out; my son was in a play at his public school which was made up of about 60 students, 4th and 5th graders singing and praising God. The text was about giving to the needy and I must confess, it was very humbling. Later on my son and I were in Wal-Mart, I gave him forty dollars to buy my Christmas gifts, but I wasn't prepared for what he told me next. He came back and told me a Miracle happened. He said he was buying my gifts and it came to sixty dollars and he did not have enough; He told the cashier he was buying the stuff for me and to take back the most expensive thing. There was a young man, maybe in his 20's, standing behind him, who, immediately told the cashier no, here's the twenty and told him Merry Christmas. As we were leaving my son pointed out the man and I went to him, "did you help my son", I asked and he said yes, "please let me give you back your twenty", absolutely not was his reply as he smiled at my son and said, I have a mother too. All I could think was God bless him......

Isn't this what it's all about, God gave it all and no matter how hard we try or how much we spend, there's nothing we can give him that He doesn't already own, except our heart. In this magical season when we have that feeling, deep down inside, that something awesome happened for us, lets open our hearts and ask Him to come in. He can replace the cold with warmth, uncertainty with definite direction and fear with security.

Our prayer today: God, I will give of myself this season and honor my friends and family with love, kindness and appreciation. In doing this, I honor You and this is all I need to strive for. I pray this in the name of Jesus. Amen.

John 10:10, *"The thief does not come except to steal, and to kill, and to destroy. I have come that they may have life, and that they may have it more abundantly."* 2 Corinthians 5:17, *" Therefore, if anyone is in Christ, he is a new creation; old things have passed away; behold, all things have become new."*

Today we're all starting a new beginning and with it comes the usual resolutions. We're setting goals and making plans, but remember, a goal won't come to pass without a realistic plan. Most of us never put much stock in what we're suppose to do, we just go through each day hoping things will get better, the devil will go away, leave us alone and we'll live happily ever after. I finally learned it doesn't work that way, I was my own worst enemy. I was allowing satan to control my life, to steal my joy. I think this is the reason I love the scripture in John 10:10, I finally realized why he was here, he didn't care about me, when he had finally beat me down to thinking I was worthless and God didn't care, he was a happy camper. What satan didn't realize was, God was always there knocking, all I had to do was open the door to my heart and let Him in. Aren't we glad we have a God who will never forsake us, who's always there waiting to pick us back up.

The word abundant means more than adequate as abundantly means profuse or overflowing. He didn't say "maybe" or "some of you", He said "you, all of us", will have life to the full and overflowing. All we need to achieve this is to invite Him in, He's not an intruder, after all, He's already done His part, it's now time for us to do ours. This year let's make our relationship with Him our number one priority, He's always had our best interest in mind. Who else can we have this much faith in? When God sets up housekeeping in our heart, here comes the joy overflowing and our more abundant life. He has a goal for us and His plan was designed a long time ago to help us be the person He created us to be. My main resolution this year is to hand Him the reins, let Him take me where He wants me to be in His timing, not mine. I'm going to relax and enjoy this journey we call life.

Our prayer today: God, this year I will put You first, I want to develop a deeper relationship with You. Thank You for sending Your Son who gave His life so I could have a new beginning. Thank You God for having my best interest in mind. Give me the patience as I wait upon Your timing and make the journey one step at a time. My prayer today, I ask You to please empty the hospitals of the sick and hurting...heal each and ease their suffering. I ask this in the name of Your Son Jesus. Amen

Through These Eyes

Ephesians 3: 20-21, *Now to Him who is able to do exceedingly abundantly above all that we ask or think, according to the power that works in us, to Him be glory in the church by Christ Jesus throughout all ages, world without end, Amen.*

We are rapidly approaching the busiest time of year. The winds, whether blustery or calm, have blown much of the leaves from the branches of our mighty and majestic trees, creating a blanket of many colors for them to stay warm as they get their much needed rest. If we slow down for just a moment, we can sense, with anticipation, the magic in the air. It's a feeling we all get this time of year, making plans to be with family, calling around trying to get the best deals for travel, decorating the house and yard, and the never ending list of names with the heading, "what to buy." This is also a time of great stress for many of us or someone we know. We tend to put so much emphasis on the cost of the gifts or the quantity of them we lose the reason of the celebration.

How many times have we been with our families or friends and one reached back in their archive of memories and brought up a Christmas of yesteryear? I can assure you nothing was mentioned concerning a gift. It was the closeness of being with each other that was remembered. Maybe we need this year to spend a little less on gifts and a little more time doing the things Jesus did while on this earth. He was constantly surrounded

249

by people except when He needed His quiet time with His Father. What we need to remember is, of all the gifts we can or will buy, the first six letters of Christmas are the most important. He should already be the center of our homes and lives. He's our Father and just like our earthly parents, He wants us to enjoy life to the abundance.

But in order for us to experience all the blessings God has in store for us, we must take a step of faith, get out of our small box and jump into the large box of God's love. Sometimes it's hard for us to fathom that by asking and believing, as His children, we will see Him do great things for us. I've learned when I ask, I start giving Him thanks and Praise, because I know it will happen, maybe not on my schedule, but He always comes through and he's never late.

Our prayer today: God, Your word says that You are bigger than I could ever imagine, and I thank You for Your bigger plans for me. Give me the strength to trust You and expect You to do great things in my life. Remind me always to give You thanks and Praise and to be a light for others to see. Help my eyes to be aware of all the needs of others around me and to loving give as You would like me to do. I ask these things in the name of Jesus. Amen

Mark 6:31, *And He said to them, "Come aside by yourselves to a deserted place and rest awhile."*

In this rushed time of the year, we might all need to set aside a little time for ourselves and God. Time to rest and catch up with the hectic pace of the day, time to put things in order. I kept a special list in my handbag for a long time of my priorities and ever so often I would have to pull it out and get myself back on track. If you will take the time to write down, and put in order of prominence, the reason you get up everyday for example, eventually things will begin to change. One day you will realize you have new habits and life is good.

I, like most of us, praise His name every chance I get, whether driving, cleaning house, grocery shopping, well you get the picture, but I wanted to share with you some special praying I was doing last evening. I was having a MRI performed and we all know they're just about as much fun as a root canal without Novocain. Since I'm claustrophobic, I was loving life. But not to be out done and let the devil have a good laugh at my expense, I seated myself, (in my mind) on a pretty spot over looking the different layers and elevations of the mountains; my Heavenly Father and I talked until my test was done. Before this ordeal got started, the technician gave me a buzzer to use if I needed him, so as I was praying he came on and asked, was I trying to get his attention, he could see my mouth moving. I said no, just having a little conversation. When it was finally over, he said, "so you were talking to yourself", I just smiled and said, I was thanking God for the beautiful scenes in the mountains and even with my eyes closed I could still see His majestic works. As his assistant was seeing me out, he said, "thank you," I said for what, "I think you know" was his reply.

When I got to my car, I paused for a minute and bowed my head. When we love our Creator and truly accept the way He made us, even a MRI slab can be our deserted, quiet place to be totally absorbed with our Father. I also thanked Him for using me to witness to this young man. By the look on his face when he said, thank you, I knew God had resurfaced in his memory bank. It doesn't matter where we are, it matters what we do. As Christians, we never know when or how He's going to use us for His Glory, so we're to be ready at all times.

Our prayer today: Thank You Lord for allowing me to witness for You. Help me to never take anything for granted, my vision, being able to speak, body movements, even the ability to think, God I owe it all to you. I pray, please touch the disabilities of all Your people and give them the knowledge to draw on their strengths. Bless each child as we celebrate Your birth this special of all holidays. Empty the hospitals of all their patients. Heal every sick and hurting body as we thank You for the gift of Your precious son, Jesus. Amen

Philippians 4:19, *"And my God shall supply all your need according to His riches in glory by Christ Jesus."*

Proverbs 3:5, *"Trust in the Lord with all your heart, and lean not on your own understanding."*

I wanted to share a story with you about a couple who learned the true meaning of being thankful for what you have and trusting in our Father God's word.

It was the week before Christmas, they had bought a new house and we all know there's hidden closing costs involved, but to get to the meat of the matter, their funds were tight. Being from the old school, one just didn't charge Christmas so they had twenty-five dollars to divide amongst their children. Soon Christmas eve had arrived. The children, after taking an aspirin so they could go to sleep, were in bed. Dad and mom sat down on the floor to wrap the meager gifts. Neither one had much to say. Dad as head of the house felt inadequate, and mom was dreading the looks of disappointment on her children's little faces. They held each other and cried.

The next morning the children were laughing as they played with their bolo paddles, western holsters and cap guns, never knowing what they might have had. Dad and mom always wanted them to have memorable Christmas's, but this one dad and mom would never forget. As grace was said around the dinner table, they realized how rich they really were. Dad said, " thank You Father God for this food which is more than we need; thank You for this house where my family is safe; thank You for my job of many years; thank You we have two vehicles in the garage so we don't have to walk; thank You for my wonderful, perfectly healthy children of which I don't know what I did to deserve; but Father God thank You in the past, present and future for sending Your son to this earth to save us all and teach us the meaning of love. Amen."

We have always judged each Christmas by that one; it taught us a valuable lesson. Whatever your difficulties, they needn't spoil Christmas, for nothing can spoil Christ! Stay focused on Jesus and seek ways to share His blessings with others, perhaps your own. Every time I doubt, every time I feel panic rising, I hear this voice whisper to me, *"I will supply your every need."*

In the last thirty days I've learn to put my priorities in order and to help me stay focused, I have made several copies of this reminder and taped it to mirrors and my refrigerator door, "God is bigger than ANYTHING I face."

Our prayer today: Father God thank You for giving me the strength to get through my trials, for my children and my job; for all my friends and family. Thank You for loving me just as I am. My prayer this day Father is please provide for and protect the children of this entire world. Keep them fed and safe from all harm. I ask these things in the name of Thy son Jesus. Amen.

We Give Thanks

I hope you had a great Thanksgiving or as some would call it, turkey day, I sure did. Now we'll be racing down to the wire, planning parties, standing in loooong lines and buying gifts. Remember Joel 3:10, *"Let the weak say, I am strong"*, we will need this in the next few weeks. I have decided that I am going to align my words with God's Word, I'm saying with each gift I buy, thank You God for coming to earth so that we might celebrate Your birth. I am troubled, yet free, I am poor, yet rich, I am weak, yet strong all because of Your word. I get so excited when I think about what a celebration we have each year, artist perform songs; streets, store fronts, houses and people are all adorned in festive decorations. The historic town of Kannapolis, North Carolina has the trees which separate the streets, decorated with clear lights and beautiful music which can be heard from the speakers placed sparsely around the buildings. It's as if you have stepped back in time. People park their cars and either ride in the horse drawn carriage or just hold hands and walk. I don't think I've ever seen anyone talking, they are simply looking everywhere and smiling. There's peace on earth if only for a little while. All of us try to out do the year before, so we fret and carry on, over extend not only our wallets but also our credit cards, when if we would stop for one moment and think, what does He want me to do. His word says for us to open our heart and invite Him in, how simple can this be? Seriously, that's all it takes. No more stress, worries or confusion, better yet as God promised Isaiah in the 26th chapter, 3rd verse that " *He will keep him in perfect peace whose mind is stayed on Him and trust in Him.*" He goes before us blocking out our enemies and removing objects that could harm us. Think about this during these next weeks and go in confidence preparing for your celebration.

Our prayer today: Thank you dear Lord for Your endless mercy and grace but from the bottom of my heart, thank You for loving me. Please help me to stop the tape that plays over again and again in my head showing me all the things I need to do. I want to place all my fears and concerns in Your hands and live in peace knowing You will fulfill Your precious promises to me....I pray heal the sick and stop the pain of the hurting, wrap Your loving arms around each of them in Jesus' name....Amen

Proverbs 31: 10, 12, 15, 20, 26, 28, 30 & 31. *"Who can find a virtuous wife? For her worth is far above rubies. She does him good and not evil all the days of her life. She also rises while it is yet night, and provides food for her household. She extends her hand to the poor, yes, she reaches out her hands to the needy. She opens her mouth with wisdom, and on her tongue is the law of kindness. Her children rise up and call her blessed; Her husband also, and he praises her. Charm is deceitful and beauty is vain, but a woman who fears the Lord, she shall be praised. Give her of the fruit of her hands, and let her own works praise her in the gates."*

Mother's Day is fast approaching and nothing, not one thing, could we give her or do for her that would even come close to the sacrifices she has made for us. Most of the efforts, sacrifices, and expressions of love our mothers have given us, would never make front page news. But what matters is not the scope of the appreciation but its genuineness.

Some of us don't have our mothers here on earth now; they're with their Heavenly Father today. This brings to mind a story I read of a teenager who lived and loved life with grand passion; She started every day with unrelenting optimism. Such is the case with Carissa, she loved soccer, basketball, friends, family and Jesus; But at the age of 12 in 2000, her whole life changed, her mother was diagnosed with cancer. During the next few years, Carissa often fed her mom, dressed her and helped her do anything she couldn't do for herself. "It was so hard to learn, " she said. "Can you imagine, a mother and daughter literally changing roles? I truly learned to be a humble servant." While her friends were out having fun, Carissa was helping her dad care for her mom. She continued to do so until the summer of 2004, when she kissed her mom for the last time. As Carissa put it, "God took her home and made her perfect." My mother was made perfect in April of '04 also. Her little thin body, crippled hands and feet are no more; she is picking flowers and dancing with the angels today. Just knowing this makes my Mother's Day very special.

On this special day, may we thank God for the mothers who have molded our hearts. As we honor them, we fulfill the truth of Proverb 31:28, *"Her children rise up and call her blessed; her husband also, and he praises her. "*

Our prayer today: Thank You Father God for our mothers, help us to always honor, love and appreciate them, not just on their special day, but everyday of the year. Bless all the mothers who can't be with their children for various reasons, may they feel in their hearts the love that is being sent through the air waves. We ask and receive these things of the name of Jesus. Amen.

As I backed out of my drive this morning, the flag I had put up for Memorial day caught my eye and I immediately thought, I must take that down this week. Just as quickly, I asked myself, why? Why do we put out the American flag only on three different holidays when it represents everything this country stands for all year?

Why do we pray to God as a last ditch effort, when He should be our first line of defense? Many men and women have died protecting and keeping this country free and Christ died to save us all. I, like most of us, have family members who have served in different branches of the military. My brother's tour lasted thirteen months in Vietnam, there he served in three major campaigns. I have an Uncle and a Cousin who both served in the Korean War. I don't have the words to truly express the debt of gratitude we owe our military personnel for what they have done and are still doing. Every time I see someone in their uniform, if I'm in speaking distance I will say to them, "thank you", if not, then I give the thumbs up. This always brings a big smile and makes me happy because they know we care. I, like you, have a heart for God therefore we have a heart for people.

The New Testament gives us some suggestions about becoming a person who gives the kind of love Christ gives. Romans 12:10, *"Be kindly affectionate to one another with brotherly love, in honor giving preference to one another."* In Romans 14:19 we are to *edify one another."* In Galatians 5:13, *"serve one another,"* Galatians 6:2, *"Bear one another's burdens and so fulfill the law of Christ."* In Colossians 3:13 we are to *"forgive one another."* 1 Thessalonians 5:11, *"Therefore comfort each other,"* and James 5:16 tell us to, *confess your trespasses to one another and pray for one another."* As I was looking for and reading these scriptures, this brought to light when Christ walked the earth. His blueprint for us to live by was and is still: His kind of love and forgiveness should go before us.

I found this poem which I thought was so fitting today because it exemplifies the love, patience and understanding we should show toward each other:

Lord, teach us the secret of loving, The love You are asking today;
Then help us to love one another; For this we most earnestly pray.

Our prayer today: Thank You dear God for our people in uniform, military, law enforcers and fire fighters. Keep them safe from all harm and bless them I pray. Take Your mighty hands and build a wall around them nothing can penetrate. I ask and receive these things in the name of Jesus. Amen

Matthew 6: 19-22 *"Do not lay up for yourselves treasures on earth, where moth and rust destroy and where thieves break in and steal: but lay up for yourselves treasures in heaven. For where your treasure is, there your heart will be also. The lamp of the body is the eye. If therefore your eye is good, your whole body will be full of light."*
John 10:10, *"I have come that they may have life, and have it more abundantly,"*

We all spend a large part of our time seeking money and possessions, but God wants us to have a different priority. The futility of riches is stated plainly in two places: here in Matthew 6:20 and in our IRS form 1040. Every year at this time, we realize that we are not as rich as we thought we were. But let's re-think this, when we put our heavenly Father in first place, we're rich beyond our wildest imagination.

In November of 1861 Julia Ward Howe wrote the words to The Battle Hymn of the Republic, "my eyes have seen the glory of the coming of the Lord." Our eyes, to me, are what make us rich. I see God everywhere because I, like you, look for Him. I must share something that simply took my breath away this past Sunday, and I sure hope you had the opportunity to witness it as well. I went to my brother's house to help him with a shelf in his garage, only to learn he had already completed it. What I didn't understand, nor made mention of, was the urgency I felt to return home.

M . E L A I N E   E L R O D

As I turned on my street, heading North, I noticed a dark sapphire blue sky with at least fifty ring-billed gulls performing an aerial ballet. As they turned, dropped and lifted, the sun made their bodies flash brilliant white, sparkling like pure silver. I quickly called my brother and asked him to step out on his deck to witness this. The more I watched, the more I was mesmerized by this show and I caught myself sharing a conversation with God. Now I finally knew the reason for wanting to come home, "seek God while He is near." One of my neighbors came over to where I was standing and said, "have you ever seen anything like this, can you imagine what a glorious sight we're going to see when the angels fill the skies?" I just looked at him, smiled and said, "we are witnessing the love of our Lord. I believe He does things like this so we'll say, Father, I know You are near and I worship You." As in John 10:10, He wants us to enjoy our life, it's our attitude and choices that makes the difference .

Our eyes are the windows to our heart. Every moment we're awake we should see our Father God everywhere and in everything we do. Our goal should be, am I on the right track, because this journey we call life, is going to end. Lets start laying up our treasures in heaven.

Our prayer today: Thank You Father God for allowing these eyes, You gave me, to see everything You put here for my enjoyment. I pray, always keep my feet on the right path, keep the windows of my heart clean and spotless. Father, we know You're the Head physician, guide the surgeon's hands as he performs a triple by-pass Friday and a cancerous prostate is removed next month. May these bodies be healed of their sickness. Protect the helpless children and elderly of this world as we ask and receive these things in the name of Jesus. Amen.

Psalm 119:45, *"For I will walk at liberty, for I seek Your precepts."* 2 Chronicles 7:14, *"If my people, which are called by my name, shall humble themselves, and pray, and seek my face, and turn from their wicked ways; then will I hear from heaven and will forgive their sin, and will heal their land."*

As this man was drawing his last breath, he took pen in hand and wrote a letter explaining his goal in writing the Declaration of Independence. "This was the object of the Declaration of Independence. Not to find out new principles, or new arguments never before thought of, not merely to say things which had never been said before; but to place before mankind the common sense of the subject, in terms so plain and firm as to command their assent, and justify ourselves in the independent stand we are compelled to take. Neither aiming at originality of principle or sentiment, nor yet copied from any particular or previous writing, it was intended to be an expression of the American mind, and to give to that expression the proper tone and spirit called for by the occasion. All of its authority rests then on the harmonizing sentiments of the day." When he was told it was July 4th, he gave in at one o'clock in the afternoon.

He felt he had to explain himself although this man was the second to hold Secretary of State office, then he was vice president, then elected as our 3rd president. When he left office there were seventeen stars on the flag, but most notably, he wrote the bill which was enacted in 1786 establishing religious freedom. Thomas Jefferson was an honorable man who loved God first and country second.

This is the time in history when the Declaration of Independence should again be shared with all, especially with our youth. The message is exceptionally appropriate today in these troubled times. This is not just a celebration for fireworks and grilling with family members. Starting with the Civil War through the present Iraq War, 1,308,174 military people have died fighting for our freedom. Freedom has never been free, it has cost our country a lot of good people and will continue to do so. Because of Thomas Jefferson we can be and are God's messengers. God is looking for a way to show a broken, battered and bruised society His boundless mercy. Aren't we happy we can gather with friends and family to celebrate this special holiday in the land of the free? May we never forget the price paid by so many? People we never knew laid down their lives for us just like Jesus. He gave His life that we might be free from sin and eternal doom. We the People should be on our knees today.

Our prayer today: God, bless this great nation of ours, which was founded on Christian principles that I believe in. Let this be a new beginning and a day to declare independence from the worries in my heart. I want to live with a positive attitude of faith. I ask this in the name of Jesus. Amen.

Proverbs 17:6 *"The glory of children is their fathers."*

Father's Day is just around the corner and those of us who are fortunate enough to still have our fathers, let's thank them for what they has meant to our lives. A father's role is to encourage his children to reach for the moon and to praise them when they've done their best. Children are mere little adults, we can't all achieve the same in life nor can they, but we all can do our best. We need to encourage each other everyday to take just one more step forward, life is so precious and it's to be enjoyed. Lets remember John 10:10.

My father went to his new home, (address Angel Way Blvd, Heaven) 16 years ago and it still seems like yesterday. He drove home the need to respect others not only by your actions but your words, that they fully understand you have total trust and confidence in them. This thinking kept me out of trouble a lot of times, I would not have disappointed my dad for all the money in the world. I remember one time I did something, don't know now what it was, but my dad said to me "baby, you broke my heart". Well we all know what came next, tears, enormous tears, buckets full, beat me black and blue, lock me in a closet but don't tell me I broke your heart.

Now that I have children of my own, I totally understand just how much his heart did hurt. I can only imagine how our Heavenly Father must feel when we blatantly go against His love for us. My father, like most men, worked hard all his life and still he was considered just a common man. If you were in need, he was there. He would till garden spots for the elderly at no charge and if they had no space to plant, he would bring food from his fields or freezer. He always had time to stop by and chat for a while, as we would say, he stopped by to put a smile on someone's face. On the day this common man died, the Tallahassee Democrat dedicated him front page. One local television station had a moment of silence and on Sunday, the local radio station dedicated their morning service to him. He never knew how many lives he touched.

Fathers, hold you children affectionately, say to them each and everyday, "I love you." These three little words mean so much, I was a grandmother before I ever heard my dad say them to me, it was on Thanksgiving day and I nearly dropped the phone. I knew he loved me by the things he did and the way he would smile at me, but it was pleasing to my ears to hear those three little words.

Our prayer today: Dear Father in Heaven, You ask that we honor our fathers and I want to start with You. Thank You for sending Your son and for being the ultimate example of what a father should be, compassionate, caring, strong and wise. Amen

Can you believe it? it's that time of year again when we have the best of intentions for our future. We're letting go of the past and we're taking on the stance of a fierce warrior, this is one battle we're going to win and some of us don't even know what we're fighting. Most of the time we set our goals so high an army would go down in defeat. I think we're all on the same page, lets see...I'm going to eat healthier foods, drink more water, exercise if it kills me, get more rest (me time), spend more quality time with my family, only use my credit card if it's a matter of life or death, stop complaining, be extra attentive and I think I'll send letters of disgust to the stations whose programs are not fit for air time. Now that I've put fingers to keyboard, I feel better, but I know this is not realistic, I must start slow and finish with a win. So when you have decided what it is you want to accomplish this next year, put it on paper, this gets it out of your head and you have something tangible to see and hold. Suddenly everything seems more real and attainable. Start each day with an affirmation, be kind to yourself, after all you're with you more than anyone else. I recently read that most people give up on their goals when success is just around the corner.

The Scripture says it this way, *"but this one thing I do, forgetting those things which are behind and reaching forward to what lies ahead, I press toward the mark for the prize of the high calling of God in Christ Jesus."* Philippians 3:13-14.

Not only do we need to let go of our bad habits and start a new life in the next year, we also need to let go of the hurt, anguish and shame that is holding us back from achieving our God given goals. Goals have never been accomplished without a plan. Henry Ford could have sat in a garage all his life, but that wouldn't have made him a car, he had to put his plan on paper and assemble all the components to achieve his goal. My plan each day starts with quiet time, just me and God. Every morning I seek His blessing knowing He already has my entire day planned, all I have to do is remember to follow His lead, not mine. So many times we think we know best and when we fail, we pray. This is the reverse of what we should do. When we let go of the past, we begin to experience the bright future God has in store for us. No matter what has happened in the past, God is a God of restoration and He will restore what the enemy has stolen from you, again, remember John 10:10.

Our prayer today: Dear God I call on You today to please help me let go of my past, put it behind me and focus on Your plan for my future. Your Son lived so that my sin would die. Your mercy is perfect and thank You for giving a me a fresh start. I ask this in the name of Your Son Jesus...Amen

Everyone I've talked with are all looking forward to a great year and well we should, this past year certainly had it's share of blessings and difficulties. We're not going to go over all the headline stories, the media has covered this enough already and there's nothing we can do now to change one thing. What we do have control over, starting today, is how we're going to look at each sunrise with its unique situations. Have you ever walked outside just before dawn? There's peace, utter peace, no dogs barking, cars racing by, no fighting or babies crying...just peace. We can have a better day but we must learn how to give, in order to receive. The old saying "Takers eat well, but givers sleep well" is only half true. According to Proverbs 11: 25 givers also eat well: *The generous soul will be made rich, And he who waters will also be watered himself.*

I once heard of a Christian businessman who hand picked something every morning to give away. He would put in his pocket a pen, a trinket or even a ten-dollar bill. As the day would unfold, he looked for someone who would be blessed by receiving a gift. "By constantly looking for an opportunity to give," he said, " I always have a wonderful day." Lets also look in 2 Corinthians 9:7, *So let each one give as he purposes in his heart, not grudgingly or of necessity; for God loves a cheerful giver.* We may not all have the means to give material things, but a kind word or smile cost nothing and does more for your soul than it does for the receiver. If we would take one day out of the week and say, "Lord, today You are in control, I'm going to smile at everyone I meet with Your love showing through," you will feel so much better and the people around you will also. It only takes one person to brighten an entire room and for this one day, no one will need an antacid. Most of us, not all, but most of us bring sickness on ourselves and infect others, we can't be happy being miserable alone, so our attitude is, if I'm going down I'm taking someone with me, when all it takes is a little less me and more of Your will Lord. Read the poem below and remember we are made in His image, so think about Him the next time you actually look in another's face.

Give as you would to the Master; if you met His searching look;
Give as you would of your substance; if His hand the offering took. anonymous

Our prayer today: Thank You God for allowing me to see another year fulfill and may I go into this New Year remembering, I may think that Christianity is about You pleasing me, but my ambition in life is going to be, to please You. My new year resolution is to live knowing the reality of eternity to come, not by the here and now experience. I pray heal the sick and hurting, ease their pains and wrap them in Your loving arms. In Jesus name I pray...Amen

Today as we approach Mother's Day this Sunday, all across this vast wonderful land we call home, mother's, step-mothers, foster-mothers, grandmothers and great grandmothers will be remembered with gifts, flowers and some will be even be barred from their own kitchens. And the mothers said..."thank You Lord for this glorious day." How nice it is to know that at least once a year we get pampered and adored. It is said the father is the weight of the family, this means he is the anchor, then I suppose this makes the mother the boat, she keeps everything afloat. Mothers give comfort through the storms of life and outside of our Almighty God, she is the greatest physician that ever lived; who else can stop pain with just one kiss.

Mother's day was started because of the love of a child, a little girl named Anna Jarvis. She loved her mother so much that when she died on May 5, 1905, she was not going to bury her and visit her grave whenever possible, no, her mother was to be remembered and so were other mothers. She started writing letters to her congressmen, asking them to set aside a day to honor mothers. In 1910, the governor of West Virginia, where she lived, proclaimed the second Sunday in May as Mother's Day and a year later every state celebrated it. After four more years President Woodrow Wilson proclaimed Mother's Day an official holiday. He said the observance serves as a "public expression of our love and reverence for the mothers of our country." Once again, this proves one person can make a difference.

For Mother's Day a few years ago my number 1 son (those of you who know me personally, know I have three sons and I have them numbered, saves time trying to remember names) wrote down some scriptures and gave them to me as my gift of which I will always cherish. The one that fits all mothers I think is Proverbs 31:31 *"Give her the reward she has earned, and let her works bring her praise at the city gate."* Mothers are special in their own right, not just because they keep the home a place of comfort but because they care. Mothers love with their hearts and our children can tear at our very core, but one little smile can mend it again, one little "I love you mom" and we forget the pain and forgive. As verse 10 of Proverbs 31 states, *"She is worth far more than rubies."*

Our prayer today: Thank you God for our mothers, help us to always honor, love and appreciate them not just on their special day but everyday of the year. Bless all the mothers who can't be with their children for various reasons. May they feel in their hearts the love that is being sent through the air waves. In Jesus name we pray...Amen

Psalm 127: 3-4, *"Behold, children are a heritage from the Lord, the fruit of the womb is His reward. Like arrows in the hand of a warrior, so are the children of one's youth."* Psalm 128:3 *"Your wife shall be like a fruitful vine in the very heart of your house, your children like olive plants all around your table."*

I remember a 17 year old boy knocking on his mother's bedroom door one night around 11:00 o'clock, I said "it's open, come on in." He never turned on the light as he sat down on the side of the bed, but I could see his face as the moon reflected brightly off the river where we lived. He said, Mom, I have something to tell you and you're going to be so disappointed in me. As I put my hand over his I told him I might be, but nothing under God's heaven could ever stop me from loving him. You're my son and for no other reason, that's enough for me. He told me he had tried marijuana and was so ashamed. As I removed the dart from my heart I asked him did he like it, he said, Oh, no ma'am and didn't see why people would actually pay for it. I told him this wasn't a mistake, it was a learning curve and I appreciated the fact he shared this private moment of his life with me.

He's now a parent and has the same open door policy with his daughter, and although being 21, she still thinks her dad walks on water.

We must make room in our lives for family. Sometimes business or social calendars need readjusting. We walk around with cellular phones in constant operation, while talking across the dinner table has become a lost art. Maybe you have told your children of God's love, but when was the last time you showed them?

Lets appreciate what God blessed us with. The dirty hand prints on the wall and the muddy socks under the bed are signs of healthy, active children who are ours but for a short while.

This brought to mind last Christmas. All my children came home, what a joyous time we had. When they went their separate ways back to their respective homes, I put the beautifully colored gift wrap and bows in the trash, a Mr. Clean sponge removed the chocolate finger prints from the kitchen walls and alcohol cleaned the storm doors, but nothing can ever erase the sounds of laughter and the memories from my heart. Can't you just see our Heavenly Father picking up behind us, putting back together our shattered lives, piece by piece and through it all, He still loves us. Starting tonight, let's try turning off the cell phones, computers and televisions, let's actually look at our family and ask, "how was your day, let's talk, I've missed our time together." Don't merely spend time with your children, invest it.

Our prayer today: Thank You Heavenly Father for the blessings you brought into my life called my children and for having enough confidence in me to properly care for them. As they keep maturing into adulthood, guide their steps, and I pray Lord keep them on the right paths. Wipe their tears and fill their bodies with Your comfort. I ask these things and accept them in the name of Jesus. Amen

Hebrews 13: 5 & 6, *"Let your conduct be without covetousness, and be content with such things as you have. For He Himself has said, I will never leave you nor forsake you. So we may boldly say: The Lord is my helper; I will not fear, what can man do to me?"*
Matthew 11:28 & 29, *"Come to Me, all you who labor and are heavy laden, and I will give you rest. Take my yoke upon you and learn from Me, for I am gentle and lowly in heart, and you will find rest for your souls."*

On Thursday, once again we will relive 9/11, this will be the 7th year anniversary of the darkest day I can ever remember happening to us. Two years ago I wrote about a documentary I came across while channel surfing one Saturday afternoon. I knew I didn't need to see this again but I couldn't turn away either. The memories of that day came back from the time the plane hit the first tower to my total exhaustion that night. My phone rang that morning and it was an account executive in Atlanta, telling me to drop what I was doing and turn on my radio. I laughingly ask him what was going on. What happened next was beyond all of America's comprehension. I do remember him saying, please don't hang up, stay with me on this. The despair in his voice was echoed throughout our universe. The one thing I had never heard that dreadful day was brought to light when I found this documentary, I guess this is the reason I can't forget it. The beeping sounds... to me, what sounded like a thousand cell phones buzzing at the same time, were actually the personal locator devices of the firemen in the rubble. Those haunting sounds, I'm sure, are with the remaining firemen and policemen even to this day.

Then we managed to survive to the second anniversary only to find out it would be as emotionally charged as the first. When at Ground Zero in New York City a group of 200 young people began reading the names of those who had died that dreadful day. The readers were the sons, daughters, brothers, sisters, nieces and nephews of the victims. The 2,792 names, precious to those who read them, brought a fresh reminder of those they had loved and lost.

A person's name represents their identify, their accomplishments and relationships. Someday our name may appear on a memorial plaque or gravestone as a mark of remembrance and honor. But there is a heavenly ledger that is the most important of all. When Jesus' followers reported their successful service to Him. He replied; "Do not rejoice in this, but rather rejoice because your names are written in heaven." Luke 10:20.

After great tragedies, many of us are challenged to put God and people first in our lives. Let's stay in the Word and take action to maintain our new perspective. A change in behavior begins with a change in the heart.

Our prayer today: Heavenly Father, thank You for loving me just the way I am and help me to always remember; it's not what we can accumulate here, but how many we can bring with us to heaven. May this country never go through another 9/11; keep us safe from all of our enemies. Ease the pain of the sick and hurting, protect the elderly and children of this entire world, I pray. I ask and receive these things in the name of Jesus. Amen

Philippians 2:3-5, *"Let nothing be done through selfish ambition or conceit, but in lowliness of mind let each esteem others better than himself. Let each of you look out not only for his own interest, but also for the interests of others. Let this mind be in you which was also in Christ Jesus."*

While I was reading this, I thought what a wonderful and better world this could be if we would rearrange the meaning of, "what about me, what's in it for me." I'll never forget when our #1 son was moving his family to another state and his dad wasn't a happy camper. As a matter of fact he didn't like it one little bit. So I asked him, "why don't you tell him how much you love him and will miss him?" Well being from the old school, you know what his answer was, "men don't do that." I had to remind him God was a man and He gave His life for him. The bond between this father and his three sons holds tighter than super glue. He learned to say I love you, I'm so proud of you, and no matter whatever happens, please remember, I'm here for you. I actually heard him apologize to our #3 son. The reason I don't remember and that's not the point. The point is he's larger than life to his boys because he let them know how important they are to him. When he realized this was what I was writing about he said, I can tell you what's in it for me, joy and gratification, knowing I'm not viewed just as the dad but as someone my boys admire and appreciate.

This is proof we can improve our relationships with anyone, a child, a neighbor or how about our boss. It starts with creating an atmosphere of peace around us, a space everyone would want to invade. Although sometimes we feel we just can't get along with certain people. God puts us with people who are different on purpose, they have a lot to give if we'll just seek to understand them. We have to focus on meeting their needs, instead of looking for what they can do for us. We must be able to overlook each other's faults and be more forgiving. If we will do these things, our lives will be much richer and we'll resolve our conflicts quicker.

And don't worry, God hasn't forgotten about our own needs. Because God is faithful, He will pour out His favor and abundance into our lives even while we're focused on blessing others. What a Savior.

Our prayer today: God, thank You for giving me my family, friends, neighbors, co-workers and all the people you have put in my life. Help me to appreciate each and everyone of them. Help me to learn from them and make it a priority to do whatever I can to meet their needs. I ask this in the name of Your son Jesus. Amen

As I backed out of my drive this morning, the flag I had put up caught my eye and I immediately thought, I must take that down this week. Just as quickly, I said, why? Why do we put out the American flag only on three different holidays when it represents everything this country stands for all year? Why do we pray to God as a last ditch effort, when He should be our first line of defense? Many, many men and women have died protecting and keeping this country free and Christ died to save us all. I, like most of us, have family members who have served in different branches of the military. I called my brother in New Jersey. His tour lasted thirteen long months in Vietnam and he served in three major campaigns. I then called my Uncle Horace in Florida who became a POW in the Korean War and told them both a heart felt, "thank you." I don't have the words to truly express the debt of gratitude we owe our military personnel for what they have done and are still doing. Every time I see someone in their uniform, if I'm in speaking distance I will say to them, thank you, if not, then I give the thumbs up. This always gets a big smile and makes me happy because they know we care. I, like you, have a heart for God, therefore, we have a heart for people.

The New Testament gives us some practical suggestions about becoming a person who gives the kind of love Christ gives. Romans 12:10, *"Be kindly affectionate to one another with brotherly love, in honor giving preference to one another.* " In Romans 14:19 we are to *"edify one another,"* Galatians 5:13, *"serve one another,"* in Galatians 6:2 *"Bear one another's burdens and so fulfill the law of Christ.* " In Colossians 3:13 we are to *"forgive one another,"* 1 Thessalonians 5:11, *"Therefore comfort each other ,"* and in James 5:16, *"Confess your trespasses to one another and pray for one another.* " As I was looking for and reading these scriptures, this brought to light when Christ walked the earth, His blueprint for us to live by, was and is still that His kind of love and forgiveness should go before us.

I found this poem which I thought was so fitting today because it exemplifies the love, patience and understanding that we should show toward each other:

Lord, teach us the secret of loving, The love You are asking today; Then help us to love one another; For this we most earnestly pray.

Our prayer today: Thank you dear God for our people in uniform, military, law enforcers and fire fighters, keep them safe from all harm and bless them I pray. Take Your mighty hands and build a wall around them that nothing can penetrate. Draw the sick and hurting close and breathe Your healing power over them. We ask these things in the name of Jesus. Amen

1 Thessalonians 5:18 *In every thing give thanks; for this is the will of God in Christ Jesus concerning you.*

This is the week we have set aside to give thanks for all the things we have and where we are today. We all have so much to be thankful for, but yet sometimes I think we take then for granted like the blessings of our Father.

I would like to take a moment and tell you about a lady, who I'm sure like most of us, dreamed of a successful life. One in which she was going to be a commercial artist, all goals could be accomplished, no need for a back-up plan. But then one day at the tender age of fifteen, she developed a degenerative eye disease. Her life as she had known it, was over, and she was frightened. Being raised to have faith in God, she learned Braille, taught herself how to count steps to get from point "A" to point "B", and to know when one door closes, He will open another. She determined in her mind He had something better for her to do, and "do" she has. She's a writer of many books and one of her top sellers is "Things I learned in the dark." She also writes and sings, attends lectures and is the founder of the Women's Ministry Net.

When we're sitting around our dinner table this Thanksgiving with our families, lets take a minute and look in the face of each one and put that picture in our memory bank; who knows we may need to replay it one day, just like Jennifer Rothschild, the wonderful person in this message. She's been married for eighteen years and has two adorable sons, none of which she has ever seen. I've been doing some thinking on this and I know in my heart if she was asked to describe her husband and boys, she would be accurate to the letter. She took lemons and made lemonade for His name sake.

Our prayer today: Thank You Heavenly Father for my family and friends, but most of all thank You for loving me. When I give thanks, this is the first thing that comes to me. Me, a person You formed in my Mother's womb, Who already had plans for my life; thank You God. Father, bless the ones who are alone, who have no home or a dinner table where to sit. For them this is a time of thanksgiving also. I give You Praise in the name of Your son Jesus. Amen

Today we will be continuing on the tenth commandment. If we can remember the first and tenth commandments, the other eight would never come into
play. Covet means to crave or desire, especially in
excessive or improper ways. The tenth doesn't tell us
that all our desires are immoral, it tells us that some
desires are wrong. When we covet what already belongs to someone else, we're wrong. We break the first
commandment when we put greed, lust and self above
God, coveting becomes idolatry.

Everyday we listen or read about people's cars being
stolen, why, because they're desired. Sometimes it's
only for a joy ride, but that's not the point, it was the
rightful property of another. We as parents, grandparents or neighbors must start listening to our young or
the gang members will. I was watching a documentary
about gangs and the number one reason a person joins
is because they have someone who "acts" as though
they care. One ex-gang member said they become your
mother and father. Well, I don't need a gang member
being a mother or father to whom God has entrusted to
me, with His guidance and love, I can put aside my own
desires until my child becomes a grown person in their
own right. If we expect to turn this world around, we
must know where our children are, the names of their
friends and where they live. Let them know they're always welcome to invade your space, the space you have
set aside just for them. Nothing ever leaves this space,

not your love for them nor their most intimate thoughts they share with you. But always make them understand, you **will** invade their space, when necessary, with absolutely no apologizes simply because you have a love for them that nothing or no one can ever take or replace.

Children learn by watching and doing as their mentors or parents do. I watched a news article which showed a mother telling her two young children to go behind a jewelry counter and pointed to actually what she wanted them to take and you could tell this wasn't the first time. They were quite good at looking around to make sure no one was there. Now the mother is in jail, who knows where the father is and the children.....well you've heard the saying a mind is a terrible thing to waste, so is a life. Unless someone intervenes, two little children are lost and will probably take more with them down their road of life.

The apostle Paul wrote many, many years ago, *"But know this, that in the last days perilous times will come: For men will be lovers of themselves, lovers of money, boasters, proud, blasphemers, disobedient to parents, unthankful, unholy, unloving, unforgiving, slanderers, without self-control, brutal, despisers of good, traitors, headstrong, haughty, lovers of pleasure rather than lovers of God, having a form of godliness but denying its power. And from such people turn away!* 2 Timothy 3: 1-5. Now wouldn't you say this is a vividly accurate description of our world today and this all deals with the mind.... the tenth commandment.

Our prayer today: Thank you dear God for giving us Your commandments to live by and the strength to do it. Thank you for the joy we feel and share each day walking in Your light. Help us to always be alert of our surroundings and to seize every opportunity to go about doing Your work. We praise You for these things in the name Jesus....Amen

Psalm 139:14, *"I praise you because I am fearfully and won-derfully made. Your works are wonderful and I know that full well."*

You can look in the mirror and say "I the wonderful creation of God," because that's the truth. There's no one else just like you, each one of God's creation are unique. He knows you, He loves you; you are the work of His hands.

Think of something you mastered or produced from your own desire, your own creativity. How did you feel about your creation? Most likely you were pleased with it, felt closeness to it, because it represented you. You wanted everyone to see it and know; this is of you. I be-lieve this is how our Heavenly Father presents us to the world; He has put His stamp on us.

There's a movement in the world today to feel good, have high self esteem and this has led many people astray; barking up the wrong tree if you will. I'm a strong proponent of feeling good but the good I'm promoting is knowing who you are in the eyes if God and feeling confident and good about how He created you and how you look through His eyes. I don't know about you but this gets me excited. Everyday I will be the best I can be for Him.

Our prayer today: Thank You Heavenly Father for creating me just the way You wanted me to be, looks and
personally. I want my light to shine so no one will ever
have to question where I stand. In the name of Jesus.
Amen.

4199531

Made in the USA
Charleston, SC
12 December 2009